THE GREAT GATSBY

*a play by
Anthony Clarvoe
from the novel by
F Scott Fitzgerald*

BROADWAY PLAY PUBLISHING INC
New York
www.broadwayplaypublishing.com
info@broadwayplaypublishing.com

THE GREAT GATSBY
© Copyright 2021 Anthony Clarvoe

Cover photo: Rudolph Valentino

First edition: December 2021
I S B N: 978-0-88145-921-0

Book design: Marie Donovan
Page make-up: Adobe InDesign
Typeface: Palatino

CHARACTERS & SETTING

The Nordics:

NICK CARRAWAY, *29*

TOM BUCHANAN, *29* / BUTLER

DAISY FAY BUCHANAN, *23* / CATHERINE / LUCILLE

JORDAN BAKER, *21* / MRS MCKEE / MISS BAEDEKER

The Crew:

MEYER WOLFSHEIM, *50* / MR MCKEE / OWL-EYES / DR CIVET / MICHAELIS

GEORGE WILSON, *35* / MR MUMBLES / KLIPSPRINGER / REPORTER / SLOANE / MINISTER

MYRTLE WILSON, *35* / MAID / GIRL IN YELLOW / STELLA / MISS HAAG / SLAGLE

JAY GATSBY, *32* / HENRY GATZ

The ensemble also plays party guests and others.

Time and place: New York City, Long Island, and various provinces of memory, 1922.

A NOTE ON THE NOTES

This project started because, on rereading *The Great Gatsby* at the suggestion of Kip Gould, Publisher of Broadway Play Publishing Inc, I said, "This is a story about white fragility," and Kip said he would love to publish that.

This is a first draft, lacking the benefit of the dozens of collaborations that are essential to making theater out of a script. The notes here and scattered throughout the play are a first attempt at my side of the many-sided conversations that go into play production. I hope they will feel inspiring, not proscriptive.

The Great Gatsby is about a hundred years old. The first fifty years or so of criticism of the novel I find all but useless; almost the only people then with access to the critical pulpit lived too close to the values and prejudices of the book to see them clearly. Only in the last fifty years or so, with the widespread availability of the resources of critical race, gender, queer, and postcolonialist theory have the truths hidden in plain sight in the story, and whirling around it, become visible and available to us. This adaptation is, I believe, both a more truthful reading of the text and a response to it from outside. Only this way, I think, can it be a useful contribution to the twenty-first century conversation about this country.

To get, literally, on the same page with this conception, the very recent Norton Critical Edition of *The Great Gatsby* (David J Alworth, editor), with Norton's usual splendid critical apparatus and vital bibliography, is strongly recommended.

CASTING NOTES

In the 1920s, magazines in which F Scott Fitzgerald published his fictions and books published by his publisher called for the purification of America from the taint of my grandparents.

My family was not the intended audience for *The Great Gatsby*. There were, and are, many Valleys of Ashes in this country. Fitzgerald described them as scenes of grotesquery and peopled them with caricatures. To my family, they were home and workplace.

The novel was written at a time when Jews, Slavs, and Italians—my family—were classed as "Mediterranean," a kind of mixed race between Nordics—northern Europeans, the "real Americans" —and Africans. White Americans were terrified that immigration and miscegenation threatened to change the color of their country. Sweeping legislation effectively ended non-Nordic immigration. The Klan was larger than ever before. White scientists claimed to prove the genetic and cultural degeneracy of Mediterraneans and Africans. Yet somehow, despite this supposed inferiority, "the colored races" were depicted as a rising force around the globe, a threat to the civilizing power of white imperialism. They were on their way, working in secret. The "passing" narrative was a popular genre. Fitzgerald responded to the spirit of his time with this novel.

The Great Gatsby meant very little to me until I found critics and other readers who confirmed my sense that Jay Gatsby is, by the racial definition of his day, not white.

Gatsby is described as having very close-cropped hair—so it won't be seen to curl, a dead giveaway—a tan face, carefully chosen mode of speech, and an extravagant style of dress. People constantly ask, "Who is he? Where did he come from?" Rudolph Valentino should have gotten the part. Even in the novel, which succeeds through a constant refusal to commit to specifics, Gatsby describes himself as "a young rajah", which is literally the title of a Valentino movie. At one point while he is being discussed, voices in the background sing *The Sheik of Araby*. *The Sheik* was the picture that made Valentino a star. As those titles suggest, Valentino, though Italian by birth, was cast as a kind of all-purpose Mediterranean exotic, a barely permissible romantic Other. The nickname Hollywood coined for him was The Latin Lover.

How that translates into contemporary terms is ripe for imagination. We're told Gatsby's birth name was Gatz. A 94-year-old Jewish friend, hearing this, said, "So he's Jewish." For me, it is very close to Gadze, a common name in both my grandfather's Croatia and in central Africa. It turns out that the Gatz family is from the Dakotas. Opportunities abound. One thing there is no point in his being is a blue-eyed blond.

The erotics of the story also deserve franker exploration than probably happened when you read it in high school. The spectrum and fluidity of desire and presentation that are expressed, or at least readily inferred, are remarkable and relevant. And if many of what in its day were perceived as transgressions seem to wind up being punished, so does a lot of the straight behavior.

I say all this as a note about casting. I hope that
actors and those who cast and collaborate with them
will believe that their identity, orientation, and their
families' culture, as they embody our national history
and culture, are vital to the full realization of the play.
The Great Gatsby is an American story, and we're
Americans now. It is public property. Let's see what
we can build from it, working as we in good conscience
must, against the grain.

DESIGN NOTES

Fitzgerald's *The Great Gatsby* was an attempt, among
other things, to use the discoveries of modernist art
in the context of a popular entertainment. Think of
the Beatles learning from modal jazz and avant-garde
electronic music. They still wanted to sell a lot of
records, and Fitzgerald wanted to sell a lot of books.
He admired Eliot and Joyce, without wanting to risk
losing his public.

So the story is a page-turner, but the imagery is often
surreal, cubist. There is yellow music; the moon
comes out of a caterer's basket; people are moths and
have animals' names. Most adaptations of the novel
naturalize its sensory world. I hope directors and
designers of this script will embrace and find theatrical
analogues for that beautiful strangeness.

In this script draft I have tried to imagine a physical
production that addresses the practical and thematic
issues of the story in theatrical terms. Other solutions
are possible and more than welcome.

The stage directions call for projection surfaces that
form a loose frame running up the sides and across the
top of a proscenium stage. They become various things
during the course of the action, but the discipline
is that they are always depictions of made images:
billboards, magazine ads, art photography. They set
the scenes by reference, at a remove. Dr Eckleburg's

famous eyeglasses, but also cars for landscape, appliances for homes, etc.—no truly natural, unmediated scenery.

When automobiles and other modes of transportation carry the characters from place to place, the performers sit or stand still while the projections flip rapidly, as if someone were skimming through a magazine glancing at the pictures and ads. The similarity in sound between revving engines and riffling pages would be fun to explore.

When the characters recount their versions of the past, their descriptions in the novel are redolent of the fictions of the earlier day. The scenic illustrations could reflect the images of the time described.

As the play begins, the billboards depict, typically for the time, a strong-jawed, well-groomed man in polo gear and two active-looking young women lounging close to each other. These are Tom and Daisy Buchanan, and Jordan Baker. The idea is that as they make their first entrances they are descending to earth from their images in the sky.

One piece of furniture is a pillowy white sofa and a bank of clouds and an automobile seat and a distant skyline.

The telephones are candlestick phones, true to the period, but with a cordlessness which is not. They might also emit light, candlestick style from earpieces and flashlight style from mouthpieces.

Duke Ellington and his Orchestra, beyond argument the greatest musical force in American history, were performing and recording in New York City *during this exact time*. And they were available to play at society parties. Fitzgerald seems to have been oblivious to the Harlem Renaissance. We need not repeat his mistake. (Fun fact: later in his career, Ellington wrote a score for a production of *Timon of Athens*, a play with some strong similarities to *Gatsby*. It's wonderful.) "The Mooche." "East Saint Louis Toodle-Oo." "It Don't Mean a Thing If It Ain't Got That Swing." "Black and Tan Fantasy." "Creole Love Call." The list goes on and on.

To my grandparents, Linda Anesi and Anthony Radalj, who made their home in the Valley of Ashes.

And to my father, for reasons he could never tell.

Scene 1.
At the Buchanans'

(A MAID *in pearl grey livery shows* NICK *in.)*

(White wicker on a runner carpet of grass.)

(In the near distance, a green light.)

*(*NICK *looks around, looks up, sees billboards above him.)*

(The billboards show three figures against blue sky: a square-jawed man in polo attire, and two women in white.)

(They detach themselves from their illustrations and descend through the clouds.)

(The women, DAISY *and* JORDAN, *lounge on the sofa.)*

(Note: DAISY *is not from the deep South. She is from Louisville, Kentucky, closer to Chicago than to Mobile, Alabama. In the novel, she is not blonde, as she is always depicted in the movies. The gold of the back of the brush she passes through her hair has been transferred to her hair itself. Her hair is dark and casts a blue shadow. To make her a golden girl is to see her as the men do, as a commodity. She is that, too, but she is not only that.)*

(Note: JORDAN *is described in the novel as tanned, lean, muscular, and athletic, with the carriage of a young cadet. That is the most the codes of the time would permit, given that* JORDAN *is a sympathetic character and lesbians and nonbinary people could not possibly count on the sympathy of Fitzgerald's audience.)*

(And NICK *will find* JORDAN *attractive. He will also be
drawn, for reasons he cannot quite articulate, to Jay Gatsby.
It is not clear how much Fitzgerald was conscious of what
seems obvious now about these characters.)*

(The man, TOM, *comes forward to greet* NICK.*)*

(Note: TOM *is not from old Eastern money. He is a product
of Chicago, and his enormous fortune, while not new, is
a generation less old than those of many of his classmates
back at Yale. There is little to say to defend him, but perhaps
there is this:* TOM *played college football at a national-caliber
level in a time before real helmets were in use. Extreme
wealth and multiple concussions have limited his intellectual
horizons and shortened his temper. He is what his culture
has made him.)*

DAISY: Nick! I'm paralyzed with happiness.

NICK: Daisy. I stopped off in Chicago for a day on my
way East. A dozen people send their love.

DAISY: Do they miss me?

NICK: The whole town is desolate. All the cars have the
left rear wheel painted black as a mourning wreath,
and there's a persistent wail all night along the north
shore.

DAISY: How gorgeous! Let's go back, Tom. Tomorrow!

TOM: We've got a nice place here.

NICK: Is that your dock, with the light at the end? I can
see it from my little place across the water.

TOM: Our dock, our lawns, run all the way from the
beach, our rose garden, our stables. Still haven't been
over all of it. Used to belong to Demaine, the oil
man. All ours now.

DAISY: This is a permanent move.

(NICK *and* JORDAN *each make quiet, skeptical noises. They notice each other doing it, glance at each other, see each other seeing, and glance away again, for now.*)

JORDAN: You're over in West Egg?

DAISY: *(Doing her mother's Kentucky accent)* My mother would say you are living on the very fringes of respectability.

NICK: Plenty of money over there.

TOM: New money.

NICK: Money is money.

TOM: And liquor is liquor, but it's safer if it's old and you know how it was made.

DAISY: So we're all New Yorkers now.

TOM: Damn fools to be anything else nowadays. Cocktails?

DAISY: You ought to see the baby.

NICK: I'd like to.

DAISY: She's asleep. She's three years old. Haven't you ever seen her?

NICK: Never.

DAISY: Well, you ought to see her. She's—

TOM: Why did you make the move, Nick?

NICK: I am learning to be a bond man.

TOM: Like everybody nowadays, who are you with?

NICK: Probity Trust.

TOM: Never heard of them.

NICK: Walter Chase's—

TOM: I have a seat on the board of one of those places myself.

JORDAN: I've had a seat on this sofa for as long as I can remember.

DAISY: Don't look at me. I've been trying to get you to New York all afternoon.

TOM: Cocktails!

JORDAN: I'm in training.

TOM: How you ever get anything done is beyond me.

DAISY: Wait! Nick, rumor has it you're engaged to a girl out West.

TOM: That's right. We heard you were engaged.

NICK: What? It's libel. I'm too poor.

DAISY: But we heard it. We heard it from three people, so it must be true.

NICK: I am not even vaguely engaged. And I have no intention of being rumored into marriage.

DAISY: No. No good can come of that.

JORDAN: You live in West Egg. I know somebody there.

NICK: I don't know a single—

JORDAN: You must know Gatsby.

DAISY: Gatsby? What Gatsby?

(DAISY's reaction is so sharp that the others all turn to look. Beat. She stands and crosses to look out.)

DAISY: (Doing her genteel English lady impression) In two weeks it'll be the longest day in the year. Do you always watch for the longest day of the year and then miss it? I always watch for the longest day in the year and then miss it.

JORDAN: We ought to plan something.

DAISY: All right. What'll we plan? What do people plan? (Catching sight of her hand, holding it out, childlike) Look! I hurted it. The knuckle is black and blue. (Herself *for a moment)* You did it, Tom. I know you didn't mean to, but you did do it. *(Going into a tough Chicago gal routine)* Eh, that's what I get for marrying a brute of a man, a great, big, hulking physical specimen of a—

TOM: I hate that word hulking, even in kidding.

DAISY: Hulking.

JORDAN: Hi, I'm Jordan, what's your name?

NICK: Nick, Nick Carraway.

DAISY: Oh my God, I always think everyone must know each other by now.

TOM: Civilization's going to pieces.

DAISY: I am merely a symptom.

(TOM hands cocktails around, including to JORDAN, who takes it for courtesy and leaves it untouched.)

(Note: JORDAN never feels entirely safe when TOM is present and is markedly different depending on whether he is there. With him, she deflects possible sexual attention by accentuating a kid-sister, tomboy performance that takes her out of what she perceives as the category of woman he wants, while not rendering her presence unwelcome to him. She is unusually fit and strong. But he is a brute. Nonetheless, she can't resist poking the bear.)

(Everybody else drinks deep.)

TOM: I've gotten to be a terrible pessimist about things. Have you read *The Rise of the Colored Empires* by this man Goddard?

NICK: Why, no.

TOM: Well, it's a fine book, and everybody ought to read it. The idea is if we don't look out the white race will be—will be utterly submerged. It's all scientific stuff; it's been proved.

DAISY: Tom's getting very profound. He reads deep books with long words in them. What was that word we—

TOM: Well, these books are all scientific. This fellow has worked out the whole thing. It's up to us, who are the dominant race, to watch out or these other races will have control of things.

DAISY: *(Doing her* TOM *impression)* We've got to beat them down.

JORDAN: You ought to live in California—

TOM: The idea is that we're Nordics. I am, and you are, and you are, and— *(A fractional pause as he looks at* DAISY's *dark hair)* And we've produced all the things that go to make civilization—oh, science and art, and all that. Do you see?

(The telephone rings, off.)

*(*TOM *exits.)*

DAISY: I do apologize for my terrible manners. Jordan, Nick is my second cousin, and he was at Yale with Tom. Nick, Jordan is—

JORDAN: What was Tom like in college?

NICK: He was very rich, even for Yale, and very strong. We were all very young.

JORDAN: So people hated his guts even then.

DAISY: But Nick didn't.

NICK: I try not to judge people.

DAISY: Lest ye be judged? What are you afraid of being judged for, I wonder. Oh, I love to see you in my home, Nick. You remind me of a—of a rose, an absolute rose. Doesn't he? An absolute rose?

NICK: I am not even vaguely like a rose.

DAISY: Darlings, I hope you won't mind if I—

JORDAN: Go.

(DAISY *exits.*)

NICK: This Mr Gatsby you spoke of is my neighbor, but—

JORDAN: Shh! Don't talk. I want to hear what happens.

NICK: Is something happening?

JORDAN: You don't know? I thought everybody knew.

NICK: I don't.

JORDAN: Tom's got some woman in New York.

NICK: Got some woman?

JORDAN: Are you surprised?

NICK: Knowing Tom, I'm more surprised that he's been depressed by a book.

JORDAN: She might have the decency not to telephone him in the evening. Don't you think?

(TOM *and* DAISY *enter.*)

DAISY: It couldn't be helped! (*Striking an attitude*) I looked outdoors for a minute, and it's very romantic outdoors. There's a bird on the lawn that I think must be a nightingale—

TOM: There's no nightingales in America.

DAISY: It could have stowed away on an ocean liner. Now he's singing away— It's romantic, isn't it, Tom?

TOM: Very romantic.

JORDAN: I thought romance went out with the war.

DAISY: Ah, the young men in uniform.

NICK: Many men with a single purpose.

JORDAN: And that purpose was Daisy.

NICK: To be honest, sometimes I miss the war.

DAISY: Tom missed the war entirely. Something about your foot?

TOM: Football injury.

DAISY: Oh, did you play football, at some college or other? I had no idea.

NICK: All American. Tom was a celebrity.

DAISY: And what was Nick known for at Yale?

NICK: Not a thing.

TOM: Nick was a sympathetic listener. Not so quick to judge people like some people.

DAISY: A politician.

NICK: I hope I'm too honest for that.

TOM: He could keep a secret.

DAISY: A father confessor.

JORDAN: Are you Catholic, Nick?

TOM: You know he's not Catholic, the butler let him in the front door.

DAISY: Not married, not engaged, not a priest.

NICK: A bachelor.

DAISY: Confirmed bachelor?

NICK: Merely habitual.

DAISY: Oh, good. You can marry Jordan, then. Handy for both of you.

(The telephone rings, off.)

DAISY: No.

JORDAN: It's like the fifth guest.

TOM: Won't be a minute. *(He exits.)*

JORDAN: So Nick, as Daisy was starting to tell you, I'm twenty-one, I'm a champion athlete, my only surviving family is one maiden aunt who does not judge me much, *(Less and less of this is addressed to* NICK*)* and who has more than enough money and a big house a day's drive away and *I have a car sitting right outside!*

DAISY: You don't understand.

JORDAN: No I do not. You could take your baby and run out of here and if that's too strenuous you could walk out and if that's too obvious you could dance.

DAISY: Stop. Bullying. Me. Nick, we don't know each other very well, even if we are cousins. You didn't come to my wedding.

NICK: I wasn't back from the war.

DAISY: That's true. Well, I've had a very bad time, and I'm pretty cynical about everything.

NICK: But your daughter.

DAISY: Yes. What about her?

NICK: I suppose she talks, and—eats, and everything.

DAISY: Oh, yes. When she was born. She was less than an hour old and Tom was God knows where. I woke up out of the ether feeling utterly abandoned, and I asked the nurse if it was a boy or a girl. She told me it was a girl, and I turned my head and wept. Just wept. I said, "All right, I'm glad it's a girl. And I hope she'll be a fool—that's the best thing a girl can be in this world, a beautiful little fool." Everything's terrible anyhow. Everybody thinks so—the most advanced people. And I know. I've been everywhere and seen everything and done everything.

JORDAN: God, you're sophisticated.

*(*TOM *enters.* DAISY *smiles and curtseys.)*

JORDAN: To be continued.

DAISY: In our very next issue.

JORDAN: Time for this good girl to go to bed.

DAISY: Jordan's going to play in the golf tournament tomorrow, over at Westchester.

NICK: Oh—you're Jordan *Baker*. I've seen your picture, in the rotogravure. Asheville and Hot Springs and Palm Beach...

JORDAN: The sporting life. Wake me at eight, won't you?

DAISY: If you'll get up.

JORDAN: I will. Good night, Mr Carraway. See you anon.

DAISY: Of course you will. In fact I think I'll arrange a marriage. Come over often, Nick, and I'll sort of—oh fling you together. You know—lock you up accidentally in linen closets and push you out to sea in a boat, and all that sort of thing—

JORDAN: *(Doing her own Chicago tough gal voice)* Ah, find another patsy, sister. I ain't marrying nobody.

DAISY: Oh, and how do you suppose you're going to get away with that?

JORDAN: Just keep beating men at golf. *(She exits.)*

TOM: She's a nice kid, really. They oughtn't to let her run around the country this way.

DAISY: Who oughtn't to?

TOM: Her family.

DAISY: Her family is one aunt a thousand years old. Besides, Nick's going to look after her, aren't you, Nick? She's going to spend lots of weekends out here this summer. I think the home influence will be very good for her.

NICK: Is she from New York?

DAISY: From Louisville. Our white girlhood was passed together there. Our beautiful white—

TOM: Did you give Nick a little heart to heart talk?

DAISY: Did I? I think we talked about the Nordic race. Yes, I'm sure we did. It sort of crept up on us and first thing you know—

TOM: Don't believe everything you hear, Nick.

NICK: I hear nothing, I promise you, nothing at all.

(The CREW *starts clearing the furniture as the lights fade down. The grass remains.)*

*(*NICK *stands alone. Automobile engine. Headlights)*

(From one side, the glow of party lights, the sounds of faint band music and laughter.)

(The green light is still there, but much smaller, distant.)

*(*NICK *stands in the moonlight and peers at the party next door.)*

(The shape of a MAN *detaches itself from the shadows.)*

*(*NICK *turns to watch.)*

(The silhouette crosses to stand facing the green light.)

(He gestures yearningly toward it.)

Scene 2:
Meet My Girl

(Then the mood and the music are obliterated by the roar of a commuter train.)

(The billboards flash advertising. Up and down the signboards on the side flash ladings and signage as seen from a train car. Lights flicker.)

(The CREW *has rolled up the lawn.)*

(NICK *stands, a little unsteadily as one does on a moving train.*)

(TOM *strides unsteadily to him.*)

TOM: Glad you could join me today!

NICK: I don't know where we're going!

TOM: Manhattan!

NICK: I know, but—

(*The screech of train brakes.*)

TOM: Come on! We're getting out here first!

NICK: Here? Why?

TOM: Want you to meet my girl!

NICK: Wait, what?

(*As if on command, the lights shift to grey daylight. The sound of the train fades away.* TOM *and* NICK *have not moved. It all happens around them. Everything comes to* TOM *as he calls for it.*)

(*With everything cleared away, the floor and everything around is grey.*)

(*The billboards' images turn more battered and down-market. One billboard shows an advertisement for an optician, a pair of spectacles and eyes, without a face.*)

(*On one side, the screens show the kinds of ads you'd see on an old gas station. Motor oil, gas prices, Coca Cola.*)

(*The rhythmic thud of earthmoving machinery.*)

(*We are in the Valley of Ashes.*)

NICK: Where the hell is this?

TOM: Hell is right. Wilson!

(GEORGE *enters.*)

GEORGE: Mr Buchanan.

TOM: Hello, Wilson, old man. How's business?

GEORGE: I can't complain, I guess. When are you going to sell me that car?

TOM: Next week. I've got my man working on it now.

GEORGE: Works pretty slow, don't he?

TOM: No, he doesn't. And if you feel that way about it, maybe I'd better sell it somewhere else after all.

GEORGE: I don't mean that. I just meant—

(MYRTLE enters.)

MYRTLE: Get some chairs, why don't you, so somebody can sit down.

GEORGE: Oh, sure. *(He exits.)*

TOM: I want to see you. Get on the next train.

(The CREW, including GEORGE, are already moving furniture in as TOM and MYRTLE arrange their assignation.)

MYRTLE: All right.

TOM: I'll meet you by the news-stand on the lower level.

(MYRTLE exits.)

TOM: Terrible place, isn't it.

NICK: Awful.

TOM: It does her good to get away.

NICK: Doesn't her husband object?

TOM: Wilson? He thinks she goes to see her sister in New York. He's so dumb he doesn't know he's alive. Come on!

(The CREW completes the transformation of the stage into the place TOM keeps in Manhattan for his and MYRTLE's trysts. It is a grotesque parody of the kind of taste we've seen in Scene 1.)

(Operetta on a phonograph)

(MYRTLE *bursts in, carrying shopping bags full of tchotchkes—throw pillows, knick knacks, etc—which she proceeds to distribute about the place as she speaks.*)

(TOM *sees about the drinks.*)

TOM: Come in, get comfortable.

(NICK *stops* TOM *as he's about to follow* MYRTLE *out, loosening his tie.*)

NICK: I should go.

TOM: No you don't. Myrtle'll be hurt if you don't stay. Won't you, Myrtle?

MYRTLE: Come on. I'll telephone my sister Catherine. She's said to be very beautiful by people who ought to know.

NICK: Well, I'd like to, but—

MYRTLE: I'm going to have the McKees come up.

(CATHERINE *and the* MCKEES *enter.* CATHERINE *has a blob of clearly artificially red hair and experimental eye makeup.*)

(*Note: the* MCKEES *are a couple played by the oldest and the youngest members of the company; in* MRS MCKEE, JORDAN's *nonbinary physicality has even greater freedom. They are sufficiently atypical as to suggest a remarkable story of survival, though, alas, they are not without prejudices of their own. They fascinate each other.*)

(*Throughout the scene, there is posing as if for photographs; showing off of purchases; considerable drinking; dancing; flirting; and a lot of petting between* MYRTLE *and* TOM. *Conversations overlap.* MYRTLE, CATHERINE, *and* MRS MCKEE *are freely expressive;* TOM *is increasingly intoxicated;* NICK *and* MR MCKEE *gravitate gradually toward each other as mutual oases of quiet and calm.*)

MR MCKEE: I'm in the artistic game. All these photographs are my work.

MRS MCKEE: He has photographed me a hundred and twenty-seven times since we've been married.

MYRTLE: My dear, most of these fellas will cheat you every time. All they think of is money. I had a woman up here last week to look at my feet, and when she gave me the bill you'd of thought she had my appendicitis out.

CATHERINE: What was the name of the woman?

MYRTLE: Mrs Eberhardt. She goes around looking at people's feet in their own homes.

MRS MCKEE: I like your dress. I think it's adorable.

MYRTLE: It's just a crazy old thing. I just slip it on sometimes when I don't care what I look like.

MRS MCKEE: But it looks wonderful on you. If Chester could get you to pose, I think he could make something of it.

MR MCKEE: I would change the light. I'd like to bring out the modelling of the features. And I'd try to get hold of all the back hair.

MRS MCKEE: I wouldn't think of changing the light. I think it's—

TOM: You McKees have something to drink. Get some more ice and mineral water, Myrtle, before everybody goes to sleep.

MYRTLE: I told that boy about the ice. These people! You have to keep after them all the time.

CATHERINE: Do you live down on Long Island, too?

NICK: I live at West Egg.

MR MCKEE: I've done some nice things out on Long Island. Two of them we have framed downstairs.

TOM: Two what?

MR MCKEE: Two studies. One of them I call "Montauk Point—The Gulls," and the other I call "Montauk Point— The Sea."

CATHERINE: I was down there at a party about a month ago. At a man named Gatsby's. Do you know him?

NICK: I live next door to him.

CATHERINE: Well, they say he's a nephew or a cousin of Kaiser Wilhelm's. That's where all his money comes from.

NICK: Really?

CATHERINE: I'm scared of him. I'd hate to have him get anything on me.

MRS MCKEE: Chester, I think you could do something with her.

MR MCKEE: I'd like to do more work on Long Island, if I could get the entry. All I ask is that they should give me a start.

TOM: Ask Myrtle. She'll give you a letter of introduction, won't you Myrtle?

MYRTLE: Do what?

TOM: You'll give McKee a letter of introduction to your husband, so he can do some studies of him. "George B Wilson at the Gasoline Pump," or something like that.

CATHERINE: Neither of them can stand the person they're married to.

NICK: Can't they?

CATHERINE: Can't stand them. What I say is, why go on living with them if they can't stand them? If I was them I'd get a divorce and get married to each other right away.

NICK: Doesn't she like Wilson either?

MYRTLE: George Wilson can go to hell!

CATHERINE: It's really his wife that's keeping them apart. She's a Catholic, and they don't believe in divorce.

NICK: I had no idea.

CATHERINE: When they do get married, they're going West to live for a while until it blows over.

MRS MCKEE: I almost made a mistake, too. I almost married a little Jew that'd been after me for months. I knew he was below me. Everybody kept saying to me: "That man is so far below you!" But if I hadn't met Chester, he'd of got me sure.

MYRTLE: Yes, but listen, at least you didn't marry him.

MRS MCKEE: I know I didn't.

MYRTLE: Well, I married mine. And that's the difference between your case and mine.

CATHERINE: Why did you, Myrtle? Nobody forced you to.

MYRTLE: I married him because I thought he was a gentleman. I thought he knew something about breeding, but he wasn't fit to lick my shoe.

CATHERINE: You were crazy about him for a while.

MYRTLE: Crazy about him! Who said I was crazy about him? I never was any more crazy about him than I was about that man there.

NICK: I have played no part in this lady's past.

MYRTLE: The only crazy I was was when I married him. I knew right away I made a mistake. He borrowed somebody's best suit to get married in, and never even told me about it, and the man came after it one day when he was out. "Oh, is that your suit?" I said. "This is the first I ever heard about it." But I gave it to him and then I lay down and cried to beat the band all afternoon.

CATHERINE: She really ought to get away from him. They've been living over that garage for eleven years. And Tom's the first sweetie she ever had. No drink for me, thanks! I feel just as good on nothing at all!

TOM: Send the janitor for some of those sandwiches. They're a complete supper in themselves.

MYRTLE: *(Playacting this, using* TOM *as a prop)* Has he told you how we met? It was on the two little seats facing each other that are always the last ones left on the train. I was going up to New York to see my sister here and spend the night. He had on a dress suit and patent leather shoes, and I couldn't keep my eyes off him, but every time he looked at me I had to pretend to be looking at the advertisement over his head. When we came into the station, he was next to me, and his white shirt-front pressed against my arm, and so I told him I'd have to call a policeman, but he knew I was lying. I was so excited that when I got into a taxi with him, I didn't hardly know I wasn't getting into a subway train. All I kept thinking about, over and over, was "You can't live forever; you can't live forever."

(MR MCKEE is showing NICK his portfolio.)

MR MCKEE: These are all my studies. Beauty and the Beast… Loneliness…

MYRTLE: My dear, I'm going to give you this dress as soon as I'm through with it. I've got to get another one tomorrow. I'm going to make a list of all the things I've got to get. A massage, and a wave, and a dog for the apartment, and a collar for the dog, and one of those cute little ashtrays where you touch a spring, and a wreath with a black silk bow for mother's grave that'll last all summer. I got to write down a list, so I won't forget all the things I got to do.

MR MCKEE: Old Grocery Horse…Brook'n Bridge…

MYRTLE: But the first thing is I want to get a dog. One of them police dogs.

TOM: What the hell do you want with a dog?

MYRTLE: I always wanted to be one of them ladies with a dog.

TOM: Where are you going to keep it? How are you going to explain it?

MYRTLE: I can say it followed me home. That happens.

CATHERINE: Don't it just.

MYRTLE: I bet Daisy has a dog.

TOM: Mrs. Buchanan does not have a dog.

MYRTLE: Daisy has a child but she doesn't have a dog. Well great. Give me a Goddamn dog and then I'll have one thing precious Daisy hasn't got.

TOM: I don't like you saying her name.

MYRTLE: Daisy! Daisy! Daisy!

TOM: Don't you say her name!

MYRTLE: I'll say it whenever I want to! Daisy! Dai—

(Making a short deft movement, TOM breaks MYRTLE's nose with his open hand. She screams, outraged.)

(CATHERINE and MRS MCKEE converge on her, offering aid.)

(TOM, sullenly drinking, strolls away.)

(NICK finds himself alongside MR MCKEE.)

MR MCKEE: Let's get out of here.

NICK: Where?

MR MCKEE: Our place is just downstairs. I've got more photographs.

NICK: What about your wife?

MR MCKEE: She doesn't mind.

(The lights fade to a yellow square on NICK.*)*

(The others are gone.)

*(*CREW *starts clearing the furniture.)*

(In passing, one CREW *hands* NICK *a portfolio of photographs.)*

*(*NICK *stands, holding the portfolio, gazing out a window.)*

*(*MCKEE *enters, in his underwear, looks over* NICK*'s shoulder at the portfolio, leans his head on* NICK*'s shoulder.)*

(They stand together in the yellow square of light.)

(Across the billboards, more yellow squares of light: an ad showing windows full of party people.)

MR MCKEE: What are you looking at down there?

NICK: Myself. Well, no. I'm imagining if I were watching this window from below and wondering about the people up here. And I'm up here. And I'm down there, looking up and wondering. I am within and without, simultaneously enchanted and repelled by the inexhaustible variety of life.

MR MCKEE: You're drunk, that's all. But you have an aesthetic sensibility.

NICK: I have been drunk just twice in my life. And the second time is this afternoon.

MR MCKEE: Come to lunch someday.

NICK: Where?

MR MCKEE: Name a place. Name a time. Let me know. *(He takes his portfolio and goes.)*

*(*NICK *looks up at the billboard people, as they fade.)*

(The sound and lights of the train on NICK.*)*

(He steps onto his lawn.)

(One of the CREW, *in their grey coveralls, and with a chauffeur's cap on his head, hands* NICK *a square envelope.*

The CHAUFFEUR *exits as* NICK *opens the envelope and removes the invitation inside.)*

NICK: *(Reading by moonlight)*
Dear Mr Carraway,
The honor would be entirely mine if you would attend a little party at my home this evening. I have seen you several times, and had intended to call on you long before now, but a peculiar combination of circumstances has prevented it. I look forward to making your better acquaintance,
Jay Gatsby

(A burst of jazz! Party lights!)

(On comes everybody, in evening dress and animal masks, dancing.)

(Someone has the Moon on a fishing pole.)

*(*NICK, *startled, dashes off.)*

Scene 3:
Party at Gatsby's

(Constant movement throughout the scene. If somebody exits as one character, they come right back on as another, with a different animal mask.)

(The movement has a kind of grace and coordination utterly in contrast to the last scene, at least early on. As the scene goes on, everything [but GATSBY*] feels as if it's gradually slowing down like an unwound clock. Things get messy later, when everyone [with one exception] is stupid drunk.)*

JORDAN: *(Who is masked)* Who brought you here?

LUCILLE: Have you met him yet?

OWL-EYES: I was driven here from the city in a Rolls Royce the color of a daisy's heart. Who has a car like that?

GIRL IN YELLOW: Trays of cocktails floating by!

MR MUMBLE: But who is he anyway?

LUCILLE: He has a machine that squeezes four hundred oranges an hour. Barrels of orange rind.

JORDAN: I went skimming across the water. I thought I might rise clear up into the air.

GIRL IN YELLOW: I walked past a room where a woman was singing whom I've heard singing at the opera. Just sitting at the piano and singing.

LUCILLE: I don't see why we always have to leave everywhere before I'm ready.

MR MUMBLE: But we're not.

GIRL IN YELLOW: Whole place lit up like a Christmas tree.

LUCILLE: I *know.*

OWL-EYES: I've never gotten lost in someone's house before.

GIRL IN YELLOW: My feet are going to pay for this tomorrow but I don't care.

MR MUMBLE: Does anyone understand why this is happening?

(NICK *enters, in white flannels, holding an animal mask.)*

(*A masked woman dances over to him and pulls off her mask. It is* JORDAN.)

NICK: Hello!

JORDAN: I thought you might be here. I remembered you lived next door.

NICK: I saw your picture in the papers! Congratulations!

GIRL IN YELLOW: Beautiful new moon.

LUCILLE: Must have come from the caterers.

MR MUMBLE: Do you come to these parties often?

GIRL IN YELLOW: I like to come, I never care what I do, so I always have a good time.

LUCILLE: When I was here last I tore my gown on a chair, and he asked me my name and address—inside of a week I got a package from Croirier's with a new evening gown in it.

JORDAN: Did you keep it?

LUCILLE: Sure I did. I was going to wear it tonight, but it was too big in the bust and had to be altered. It was gas blue with lavender beads. Two hundred and sixty-five dollars.

GIRL IN YELLOW: There's something funny about a fellow that'll do a thing like that. He doesn't want any trouble with anybody.

NICK: Who doesn't?

GIRL IN YELLOW: Gatsby.

MR MUMBLE: Somebody told me they thought he killed a man once.

LUCILLE: I don't think it's so much that; it's more that he was a German spy during the war.

MR MUMBLE: I heard that from a man who knew all about him, grew up with him in Germany.

LUCILLE: Oh, no, it couldn't be that, because he was in the American army during the war.

GIRL IN YELLOW: You look at him sometimes when he thinks nobody's looking at him. I'll bet he killed a man.

NICK: I've still never met him. It's making me uneasy.

OWL-EYES: (Holding out a handsomely bound book) What do you think of this?

JORDAN: About what?

OWL-EYES: It's real.

JORDAN: The book?

OWL-EYES: They're all real. You needn't ascertain it. I've ascertained it.

JORDAN: His books?

OWL-EYES: Got a library full of them. Absolutely real— have pages and everything. I thought they'd be a nice durable cardboard. Matter of fact, they're absolutely real. Pages and— See! It's a bona-fide piece of printed matter. It's a triumph. What thoroughness! What realism!

NICK: Maybe you should put it back.

OWL-EYES: I see. You think if one brick is removed the whole edifice will collapse.

NICK: And you? Who brought you? Or did you just come?

OWL-EYES: I was brought.

GIRL IN YELLOW: Most people were brought.

OWL-EYES: We were brought by a woman named Roosevelt. Mrs Claud Roosevelt. Do you know her? We met her somewhere last night. I've been drunk for…

GIRL IN YELLOW: For about a week now. Yes.

OWL-EYES: And I thought it might sober me up to sit in a library.

JORDAN: Did it?

OWL-EYES: A little bit, I think. I can't tell yet. We've only been here an hour. Did I tell you about the books? They're real. They're—

NICK: You told us.

JORDAN: Dance with me. There's a college boy coming my way and his conversation before was downright obstetrical.

(NICK *and* JORDAN *dance together.*)

(*As they do, the guests who are members of the* CREW *surround the one of their number who has been, to this point, clad only in his coverall and cap like the others. As he stands with his back to us, they lovingly remove the coverall, revealing as from a cocoon a butterfly a gorgeously clad young man. As he turns, his good looks reveal him to be not Nordic—whatever that may be—but Mediterranean. That was the racial term in 1922. He goes by the name* JAY GATSBY. *He crosses to* NICK, *smiling.*)

GATSBY: Your face is familiar. Weren't you in the Third Division during the war?

NICK: Why, yes. I was in the Ninth Machine Gun Battalion.

GATSBY: Seventh Infantry. I knew I'd seen you somewhere before.

NICK: You were at the Marne?

GATSBY: Hm. Argonne Forest?

(*Note: The Meuse-Argonne Offensive was and is to this day the deadliest battle in American military history. Sudden, grotesque death on all sides for days on end. That these two were there then and alive now is in a way all they will ever need to know about each other.*)

(NICK *raises his glass, and* GATSBY *his.*)

NICK: Absent friends.

(GATSBY *and* NICK *drink.*)

GATSBY: I've just bought a hydroplane. I'm going to try it out in the morning. Want to go with me, old sport? Just near the shore along the Sound.

NICK: What time?

GATSBY: Any time that suits you best.

NICK: What's your—

JORDAN: Having a gay time now?

NICK: Much better. This is an unusual party for me. I haven't even seen the host. I live over there—and this man Gatsby sent over his chauffeur with an invitation.

GATSBY: I'm Gatsby.

NICK: What! Oh, I beg your pardon.

GATSBY: I thought you knew, old sport. I'm afraid I'm not a very good host.

BUTLER: Chicago is calling on the wire.

GATSBY: Will you both excuse me? If you want anything just ask for it. I will rejoin you later.

NICK: He's not at all what I expected.

JORDAN: What were you expecting?

NICK: Who is he? Do you know?

JORDAN: He's just a man named Gatsby.

NICK: Where is he from, I mean? And what does he do?

JORDAN: Now you've started on the subject.

NICK: If you had told me he sprang from the swamps of Louisiana or from the Lower East Side of New York—

JORDAN: You think he's a Negro, or a Cajun, or a Jew?

NICK: I mean that would be more comprehensible—in my experience—he's my age! Men my age don't drift coolly out of nowhere and buy a palace on Long Island Sound!

JORDAN: Anyhow, he gives large parties, and I like large parties. They're so intimate. At small parties there isn't any privacy.

BUTLER: I beg your pardon. Miss Baker? I beg your pardon, but Mr Gatsby would like to speak to you alone.

JORDAN: With me?

BUTLER: Yes, madame.

JORDAN: Well, now.

MR MUMBLE: You promised!

LUCILLE: Whenever you see I'm having a good time you want to go home.

GIRL IN YELLOW: Never heard anything so selfish in my life.

NICK: What's going on?

GIRL IN YELLOW: They're having a fight. He says he's her husband.

NICK: A lot of women seem to be having fights with men who say they are their husbands.

LUCILLE: We are always the first ones to leave.

GIRL IN YELLOW: So are we.

OWL-EYES: Well, we're almost the last tonight. The orchestra left half an hour ago.

JORDAN: I've just heard the most amazing thing. It was—simply amazing. But I swore I wouldn't tell it and here I am tantalizing you. Please come and see me…

(Now that it's time to go, people have donned hats in the shape of cars. They run into and bump and bash each other as they try to exit. Some fall down, and lie where they have fallen.)

JORDAN: *(As she is borne away)* Phone book… Under the name of Miss Sigourney Howard… My aunt…

NICK: Sorry to stay so late.

GATSBY: Don't mention it.

NICK: And so sorry that I didn't know who you were, before.

GATSBY: Don't give it another thought, old sport. And don't forget we're going up in the hydroplane tomorrow morning, at nine o'clock.

BUTLER: Philadelphia wants you on the phone, sir.

GATSBY: All right, in a minute. Tell them I'll be right there…good night.

NICK: Good night.

GATSBY: Good night, old sport.

(The sound of a fender bender, horns, voices.)

NICK: Good night.

(NICK tries to walk away and finds himself among the fallen. He joins them, supine.)

OWL-EYES: I think that I have gone into a ditch!

NICK: How did it happen?

OWL-EYES: I seem to have been in an automobile. I know nothing whatever of mechanics.

GIRL IN YELLOW: Oh the stars.

LUCILLE: I *know*.

NICK: But how did it happen? Did you run into the wall?

OWL-EYES: Don't ask me. I know very little about driving—next to nothing. It happened, and that is all I know. And all I need to know.

NICK: Well, if you're a poor driver you oughtn't to try driving at night.

OWL-EYES: But I wasn't even trying. I wasn't even trying. *(He discovers a shoe and studies it.)* I seem to have lost a...wheel. In the collision.

NICK: Do you want to commit suicide? You're lucky it was just a wheel! A bad driver and not even trying!

OWL-EYES: You don't understand. I wasn't driving. There was another man in the car.

MR MUMBLE: Wha's matter? Did we run outa gas?

OWL-EYES: Look! One of the...wheels came off!

MR MUMBLE: At first I din' notice we'd stopped. Wonder'ff tell me where there's a gas'line station?

NICK: Your wheel and your car are no longer joined by any physical bond.

MR MUMBLE: Back out. Put her in reverse.

NICK: But the wheel's off!

MR MUMBLE: No harm in trying.

(More people are lying on the ground by now.)

(Headlights rise and become the midsummer morning sun.)

(Someone starts to play a ukulele.)

(The billboards show ads featuring beach umbrellas with Cinzano logos etc.)

(Some people find themselves in swim attire. They wander on that way or just lose their party clothes. Towels are spread.)

LUCILLE & GIRL IN YELLOW: *(Singing quietly in harmony)*
By the sea, by the sea
By the beautiful sea
You and I you and I
Oh how happy we'll be

(And if, just here, a model hydroplane could buzz by overhead, perhaps held aloft on another fishing pole like the moon, well, that would be fabulous.)

OWL-EYES: *(Pointing to the plane)* Hail to thee, blithe spirit!

(Everybody looks up at the hydroplane, points, follows it, turning their heads in unison and sighing, Ah!)

(The ukulele continues to strum.)

OWL-EYES: *(Reading aloud)*
"Away! away! for I will fly to thee,
Not charioted by Bacchus and his pards,
But on the viewless wings of Poesy…"

(GATSBY enters, and takes in the day that he has made.)

Scene 4:
Two Drives

(NICK and the CREW are lying on the beach.)

GATSBY: Good day, old sport.

NICK: Mr Gatsby. Many thanks for the use of the beach.

GATSBY: I'm glad to see you're using it. Take a dip in the swimming pool if you like. You'd be doing me a favor, I haven't used it once this summer. Then later you're having lunch with me in town. We can ride up together. Would that suit you?

(Everybody sighs, gets up, and clears the stage as NICK gets dressed.)

GATSBY: Look here, old sport. What's your opinion of me, anyhow?

(The roar of the most powerful automobile engine we've heard yet.)

(The billboards show ads for a gleaming, luxurious Rolls, yellow paint and chrome and much glass and many mirrors.)

(GATSBY speaks loudly as he drives himself and NICK.)

GATSBY: I'm going to tell you something about my life. I don't want you to get a wrong idea of me from all these stories you hear. What's the latest?

NICK: One time you killed a man because he had found out that you are the nephew of the Kaiser and second cousin to the devil himself.

GATSBY: I'll tell you God's truth. I am the son of some wealthy people in the Middle West—all dead now. I was brought up in America but educated at Oxford, because all my ancestors have been educated there for many years. It is a family tradition.

NICK: What part of the Middle West?

GATSBY: San Francisco.

(A flummoxed look from NICK, which GATSBY doesn't see.)

GATSBY: My family all died and I came into a good deal of money. After that I lived like a young rajah in all the capitals of Europe—Paris, Venice, Rome—collecting jewels, chiefly rubies, hunting big game, painting a little, things for myself only, and trying to forget something very sad that had happened to me long ago. Then came the war, old sport. It was a great relief, and I tried very hard to die, but I seemed to bear an enchanted life.

(The drive has been downtown, not uptown as with TOM. Very different feeling. Signage and imagery are "foreign" and "exotic".)

(By now the CREW has set up a café table with a few chairs.)

(GATSBY and NICK are seated at the table.)

GATSBY: I accepted a commission as first lieutenant when it began. In the Argonne Forest I took two machine gun detachments a half mile ahead of the infantry. We stayed there two days and two nights, a hundred and thirty men with sixteen Lewis guns, and when the infantry came up at last they found the insignia of three German divisions among the piles of dead. I was promoted to be a major, and every Allied government gave me a decoration—even Montenegro, little Montenegro. Look. *(He produces souvenirs from his pockets and holds them out.)*

NICK: "Orderi di Danilo. Montenegro, Nicolas Rex."

GATSBY: Turn it over.

NICK: "Major Jay Gatsby, For Valour Extraordinary."

GATSBY: Here's another thing I always carry. A souvenir of Oxford days. It was taken in Trinity Quad—the man on my left is now the Earl of Dorcaster.

NICK: So it's all true!

GATSBY: I'm going to make a big request of you today, so I thought you ought to know something about me. I didn't want you to think I was just some nobody. You see, I usually find myself among strangers because I drift here and there trying to forget the sad thing that happened to me. You'll hear about it this afternoon.

NICK: At lunch?

GATSBY: No, this afternoon. You and Miss Baker are having tea at the Plaza.

NICK: How do you…are you in love with Miss Baker?

GATSBY: No, old sport, I'm not. But Miss Baker has kindly consented to speak to you about this matter. Look here, I'm afraid I've made you a little angry.

NICK: I don't like mysteries. And I don't understand why you won't come out frankly and tell me what you want. Why has it all got to come through Miss Baker?

GATSBY: Oh, it's nothing underhand. Miss Baker's a great sportswoman, you know, and she'd never do anything that wasn't all right. Highball?

NICK: So this is—I thought perhaps, but it's a…I don't mean to be naïve…

GATSBY: Yes, they serve liquor here.

NICK: Do they ever get raided? You read about these places getting raided.

GATSBY: You see that man over there? That's the Commissioner of Police. *(Waving genially)* I was able to do him a favor once. He sends me a Christmas card every year.

NICK: Oh my Lord, and that's my boss.

GATSBY: Your boss?

NICK: Walter Chase.

GATSBY: You're with Probity Trust?

NICK: Yes. Why? Have you heard something about—

GATSBY: You can't believe everything you hear, old sport.

NICK: Oh, I don't know, I'm beginning to believe that once you slide over that bridge, anything can happen, anything at all. Even you, Mr. Gatsby.

GATSBY: Even me. I wonder at it myself sometimes.

WOLFSHEIM: And look who it is!

GATSBY: Mr. Carraway, this is my friend Mr Wolfsheim.

(Note: MEYER WOLFSHEIM, *in the novel, is a work of anti-Semitism so appalling that even Fitzgerald evidently came to feel queasy about it later in life. He's a gangster. He's Jewish. There were Jewish gangsters. The only thing left from the book is his dialogue and his cufflinks.* STELLA, *his assistant, hovers nearby.)*

WOLFSHEIM: So that business with—

GATSBY: Sure—

WOLFSHEIM: What do you think I did? I handed the money to Katspaugh—

GATSBY: To Katspaugh, brilliant—

WOLFSHEIM: And I said, "All right, Katspaugh, don't pay him a penny till he shuts his mouth."

GATSBY: And did he shut it?

WOLFSHEIM: He shut it then and there. Mr Carraway, pleased to make your acquaintance.

STELLA: Highballs?

GATSBY: I didn't expect to see you here.

WOLFSHEIM: This is a nice restaurant here. But I like across the street better.

GATSBY: Yes, highballs, thanks, Stella. It's too hot for me over there.

WOLFSHEIM: Hot and small—yes, but full of memories.

NICK: What place is that?

WOLFSHEIM: The old Metropole. Filled with faces dead and gone. Filled with friends gone now forever. I can't forget so long as I live the night they shot Rosy Rosenthal there. It was six of us at the table, and Rosy had eat and drunk a lot all evening. When it was almost morning the waiter came up to him with a funny look and says somebody wants to speak to him outside. "All right," says Rosy, and begins to get up, and I pulled him down in his chair. "Let the bastards come in here if they want you, Rosy, but don't you, so help me, move outside this room." It was four o'clock in the morning then, and if we'd of raised the blinds we'd of seen daylight.

NICK: Did he go?

WOLFSHEIM: Sure he went. He turned around in the door and says, "Don't let that waiter take away my coffee!" Then he went out on the sidewalk, and they shot him three times in his full belly and drove away.

NICK: I remember now. Four of them were sent to the electric chair.

WOLFSHEIM: Five, with Becker. I understand you're looking for a business connection.

(NICK *is frankly terrified by this point.* GATSY *has registered this.*)

GATSBY: Meyer?

(A look passes between GATSBY *and* WOLFSHEIM.*)*

GATSBY: This isn't the man.

WOLFSHEIM: No?

GATSBY: This is just a friend. Let's talk about that some other time.

WOLFSHEIM: I beg your pardon. I had a wrong man.

(STELLA *signals to* GATSBY.*)*

GATSBY: I should make a call. Excuse me. *(He exits.)*

WOLFSHEIM: Fine fellow, isn't he? Handsome to look at and a perfect gentleman.

NICK: Yes.

WOLFSHEIM: He's an Oxford man. He went to Oxford College in England.

NICK: Have you known Gatsby for a long time?

WOLFSHEIM: Several years. I made the pleasure of his acquaintance just after the war. But I knew I had discovered a man of fine breeding after I talked with him an hour. I said to myself, "There's the kind of man you'd like to take home and introduce to your mother and sister." I see you're looking at my cuff buttons. Finest specimens of human molars.

NICK: Well! That's a very interesting idea.

WOLFSHEIM: Yeah. Yeah, Gatsby's very careful about women. He would never so much as look at a friend's wife.

(GATSBY *enters.*)

WOLFSHEIM: I have enjoyed making your acquaintance, and I'm going to run off from you two young men before I outstay my welcome.

GATSBY: Don't hurry, Meyer.

WOLFSHEIM: You're very polite, but I belong to another generation. You sit here and discuss your sports and your young ladies and your—As for me, I am fifty years old, and I won't impose myself on you any longer. (*He exits.*)

GATSBY: He becomes very sentimental sometimes. This is one of his sentimental days. He's quite a character around New York—a denizen of Broadway.

NICK: Who is he, anyhow, an actor?

GATSBY: No.

NICK: A dentist?

GATSBY: Meyer Wolfsheim? No, he's a gambler. He's the man who fixed the World's Series back in 1919.

NICK: Fixed the World's Series? I remember, of course, I know that it happened, but it never occurred to me that it's something that someone had done. How did he happen to do that?

GATSBY: He just saw the opportunity.

NICK: Why isn't he in jail?

GATSBY: They can't get him, old sport. He's a smart man.

(TOM *enters.*)

TOM: Nick!

NICK: Give me a minute. I've got to say hello to someone.

TOM: Where've you been? Daisy's furious, you haven't called up.

NICK: Mr Buchanan. This is Mr Gatsby—

TOM: How've you been, anyhow? How'd you happen to come this far to eat?

(GATSBY *exits.*)

NICK: I've been having lunch with…Mr Gatsby.

(*But* GATSBY *is gone. Everybody is gone but* NICK, *and…*)

(*…sitting at the table, proper as can be,* JORDAN.)

NICK: Jordan?

JORDAN: Hi, Nick. So you had lunch with Gatsby.

NICK: I did. He told me his whole true life story.

JORDAN: What was that like?

NICK: It was like flipping through a dozen stories from romance magazines.

JORDAN: You didn't believe him?

NICK: I'm trying not to judge. What do you think he is?

JORDAN: I think Gatsby is whatever he thinks you want. There's a story I need to tell you.

NICK: About…

JORDAN: Let's go for a drive.

(JORDAN *crosses to sit on the sofa.* NICK *follows and joins her.*)

(An automobile engine that becomes unreal as she drives them into the past.)

NICK: To…

JORDAN: So it's 1917. Louisville, Kentucky. I am going past the biggest lawn of the biggest house in Louisville, which belonged to the family of the most popular girl in Louisville, and her name was Daisy Fay.

(To the sound of a fanfare of telephones, enter DAISY, *strolling, in white.)*

JORDAN: She was just eighteen, two years older than me, and all day long her telephone rang with lovesick young officers calling from Camp Taylor, begging for a little of her time. That morning when I saw her, she was with a lieutenant I had never seen before.

(Trotting in to join DAISY *is a young lieutenant:* GATSBY.*)*

JORDAN: They were so engrossed in each other that she didn't see me until they were five feet away.

DAISY: Jordan Baker! Wait a minute?

JORDAN: Daisy? Hello! Hi!

DAISY: Are you going to the Red Cross and make bandages?

JORDAN: I am.

DAISY: Would you tell them that I can't come today?

*(*DAISY *and* GATSBY *walk off, gazing at each other.)*

JORDAN: He looked at her in a way that everybody wants to be looked at sometime. It seemed so romantic I remembered it ever since. By the next year wild rumors were circulating about her—

*(*DAISY *dances on…)*

JORDAN: How her mother caught her packing a bag one winter night to go to New York and say goodbye to a soldier who was going overseas.

(...*and stumbles*...)

JORDAN: Her family stopped her.

(...*and falls to her knees.*)

JORDAN: After that she didn't play around with soldiers anymore.

(DAISY *picks herself up*...)

JORDAN: By the next autumn she was gay again, gay as ever.

(...*and prances off.*)

JORDAN: She had a debut after the Armistice, and by June she was engaged to Tom Buchanan of Chicago, with more pomp and circumstance than Louisville ever knew before. He came down with a hundred people in four private railroad cars, and hired a whole floor of the Seelbach Hotel, and he gave her a string of pearls valued at three hundred and fifty thousand dollars. I was bridesmaid.

(DAISY *staggers in*...)

JORDAN: Half an hour before the bridal dinner, she came into my room, lovely as the June night—and as drunk as a monkey. She had a bottle of Sauterne in one hand and a letter in the other.

DAISY: 'Gratulate me. Never had a drink before, but oh how I do enjoy it.

JORDAN: Daisy? What's the matter?

DAISY: (*Holding out a sumptuous string of pearls*) Here, deares'. Take 'em downstairs and give 'em back to whoever they belong to. Tell 'em all Daisy's change' her mine. Say: "Daisy's change' her mine!"

(DAISY, *sobbing, falls onto the sofa into* JORDAN's *arms. A long moment when* JORDAN *holds her,* DAISY's *head to her chest*...)

JORDAN: I locked the door and got her into a cold bath. She wouldn't let go of the letter. She squeezed it up into a wet ball, and she only let me leave it in the soap-dish when she saw it was coming to pieces like snow. But she didn't say another word.

(DAISY *slips out of* JORDAN's *arms, collects herself, and walks calmly out.*)

JORDAN: I gave her spirits of ammonia and put ice on her forehead and hooked her back into her dress, and half an hour later, the pearls were around her neck and the incident was over. Next day at five o'clock she married Tom Buchanan without so much as a shiver.

(DAISY *and* TOM, *bride and groom, process across and off.*)

JORDAN: They left on a three months' trip to the South Seas. I saw them in Santa Barbara when they came back, and I thought I'd never seen a girl so mad about her husband.

(DAISY *enters, more tentatively than we've seen her.*)

DAISY: Where's Tom gone?

JORDAN: I don't know, dearest.

DAISY: (*Singing to the old nursery tune; this is the first time [chronologically] we've heard her do one of her routines*)
Oh where, oh where has my little Tom gone
Oh where, oh where can he be…

(TOM *enters and* DAISY *runs to embrace him, touching his face and hair tenderly.* JORDAN *laughs softly and shakes her head as they go, still embraced. Then her face turns grim. The sound of the automobile engine [*JORDAN *has, on some level, been driving all this time] gets louder and higher as…*)

JORDAN: That was in August. A week after I left Santa Barbara, Tom ran into a farm wagon on the Ventura road one night, and ripped a front wheel off his car. The girl who was with him got into the papers, too, because her arm was broken. She was one of the chambermaids in the Santa Barbara Hotel.

(A blare of horns, a shriek of tires. NICK *holds on tight.)*

NICK: You're a rotten driver yourself! Either you ought to be more careful, or you oughtn't to drive at all.

JORDAN: I am careful.

NICK: No, you're not.

JORDAN: Well, other people are.

NICK: What's that got to do with it?

JORDAN: They'll keep out of my way. It takes two to make an accident.

(The engine dies. JORDAN *and* NICK *sit there.)*

NICK: Suppose you met somebody just as careless as yourself.

JORDAN: I hope I never will. I hate careless people. That's why I like you.

*(*JORDAN *moves closer to* NICK. *Throughout what follows, the more they talk about* GATSBY *and* DAISY, *the more intimately excited they feel. About whom they feel most passionately is an open question, one that neither one could scarcely ask, much less answer.)*

NICK: You say you hate careless people, but…you love Daisy.

JORDAN: I—

NICK: She's your friend.

JORDAN: Daisy Buchanan has turned into the most careful person I know. She and Tom moved with a fast crowd in Chicago, young and rich and wild, but she came out with a perfect reputation. No little indiscretions. Never a rumor again.

NICK: Maybe she just doesn't go in for indiscretions.

JORDAN: Maybe. There's something in that voice of hers… But the mask never slips. Until the other night, when she heard me say the name Gatsby.

NICK: You asked me if I knew him.

JORDAN: After you went home, she came into my room and woke me up.

(DAISY *crosses in, one last time.*)

DAISY: What Gatsby?

JORDAN: *(To* NICK*)* I was half asleep.

DAISY: What Gatsby?

JORDAN: *(To* NICK*)* I described him.

DAISY: *(A strange voice, but her own)* It must be the man I used to know.

(*As* DAISY *goes…*)

JORDAN: It wasn't until then that I learned that Gatsby was that lieutenant, all those years ago.

NICK: It's a strange coincidence.

JORDAN: It isn't a coincidence at all. Gatsby bought that house so he would be just across the bay from her. He's read a Chicago paper for years, on the chance of seeing her name. He found out they moved here, and bought that house.

(*It is night by now.*)

(NICK'*s lawn appears.*)

(GATSBY *stands on it, looking at the green light in the distance.*)

JORDAN: Now he wants to know: will you invite Daisy to your home some afternoon, and let him come over?

NICK: Did I have to know all this before he could ask such a little thing?

JORDAN: He's afraid. He's waited so long. Daisy's your cousin, Tom's your friend. He thought you might be offended.

NICK: Why didn't he ask you to arrange a meeting?

JORDAN: He wants her to see his house, and your house is right next door. I think he half expected her to wander into one of his parties some night, but she never did. Then he began asking people if they knew her, and I was the first one he found. It was that night he sent for me at his dance.

NICK: Does Daisy want to see him?

JORDAN: She's not to know about it. Gatsby doesn't want her to know. You're just supposed to invite her to tea.

NICK: He waited five years and bought a mansion so he could come over one day and see her in a stranger's garden?

JORDAN: Not a stranger. He must think you're his friend, too.

NICK: What do you think?

JORDAN: I think ... Daisy ought to have something in her life.

(JORDAN *turns her face to* NICK's. *So they kiss.*)

(*The lights fade on them.*)

(GATSBY *still stands, in the moonlight and the glow from his house.*)

(*The sound of an automobile approaching, stopping. Door. Driving away*)

(NICK *crosses to join* GATSBY.)

NICK: Your place looks like the World's Fair.

GATSBY: Does it? I have been glancing into some of the rooms. Let's go to Coney Island, old sport. In my car.

NICK: It's too late for me.

GATSBY: Well, suppose we take a plunge in the swimming pool? I haven't made use of it all summer.

NICK: I talked with Miss Baker. I'm going to call up Daisy tomorrow and invite her over here to tea.

GATSBY: Oh, that's all right. I don't want to put you to any trouble.

NICK: What day would suit you?

GATSBY: What day would suit you? I don't want to put you to any trouble, you see.

NICK: How about the day after tomorrow?

GATSBY: I want to get the grass cut.

NICK: But your grass is… Oh, you mean my grass.

GATSBY: There's another little thing.

NICK: Would you rather put it off for a few days?

GATSBY: Oh, it isn't about that. At least— Why, I thought—why, look here, old sport, you don't make much money, do you?

NICK: Not very much.

GATSBY: I thought you didn't, if you'll pardon my— You see, I carry on a little business on the side, a sort of sideline, you understand. And I thought that if you don't make very much— You're selling bonds, aren't you, old sport?

NICK: Trying to.

GATSBY: Well, this would interest you. It wouldn't take up much of your time and you might pick up a nice bit of money. It happens to be a rather confidential sort of thing.

NICK: I've got my hands full.

GATSBY: You wouldn't have to do any business with Wolfsheim.

NICK: I'm just having two people over for tea. It's a small thing.

GATSBY: Not to me. I suppose I am indebted to you, then.

NICK: You have been my host. I'm returning the favor. All right?

GATSBY: All right. Good night, old sport.

(The lights fade.)

(When they come up again, it is the light of a rainy summer afternoon.)

Scene 5:
Reunion

(The sound of rain)

(The CREW sets up NICK's sitting room for tea.)

(There is, among the sparse furnishings, an old clock on a shelf.)

(A CREW member runs a lawn mower up the grass.)

(NICK and GATSBY watch all this bustle.)

GATSBY: Is everything all right?

NICK: The grass looks fine, if that's what you mean.

GATSBY: What grass? Oh, the grass in the yard. Looks very good. One of the papers said they thought the rain would stop about four. Have you got everything you need in the shape of—of tea?

NICK: Will this do?

(There's a tray going by in the hands of one of the CREW. It's sparse, but it's tea and cakes.)

GATSBY: Of course, of course! That's fine…old sport. *(Beat)* I'm going home.

NICK: Why's that?

GATSBY: Nobody's coming to tea. It's too late! I can't wait all day.

NICK: Don't be silly; it's just two minutes to four.

(The sound of an engine.)

(NICK crosses to meet DAISY.)

(GATSBY has vanished.)

DAISY: Is this absolutely where you live, my dearest one? Are you in love with me? Why did I have to come alone?

(NICK looks around, mystified, at his depopulated room.)

NICK: Well, that's funny.

DAISY: What's funny?

(A knock)

NICK: Come in?

(GATSBY enters, pale as death.)

(DAISY and GATSBY stare at each other for an extraordinary time.)

DAISY: I certainly am awfully glad to see you again.

(GATSBY makes his way over to the shelf and leans against it.)

GATSBY: We've met before.

(The clock takes this moment to tilt dangerously at the pressure of GATSBY's head, whereupon he turns and catches it with trembling fingers, and sets it back in place.)

GATSBY: I'm sorry about the clock.

NICK: It's an old clock. There's tea, I'll get some tea, if anybody wants some tea. *(He exits.)*

DAISY: We haven't met for many years.

GATSBY: Five years next November.

(NICK returns with tea things.)

NICK: Tea. There's the tea. Will you excuse me?

GATSBY: Where are you going?

NICK: I'll be back.

GATSBY: I've got to speak to you about something before you go.

(GATSBY and NICK huddle away from DAISY.)

GATSBY: Oh, God!

NICK: What's the matter?

GATSBY: This is a terrible mistake, a terrible, terrible mistake.

NICK: You're just embarrassed, that's all. Daisy's embarrassed too.

GATSBY: She's embarrassed?

NICK: Just as much as you are.

GATSBY: Don't talk so loud.

NICK: You're acting like a little boy. Not only that, but you're rude. Daisy's sitting in there all alone.

(GATSBY squares his shoulders and heads back to DAISY. They are only visible in silhouette, sitting facing each other, very close.)

(NICK stands on his lawn, holding a telephone. He dials.)

(JORDAN appears, with a telephone.)

NICK: They're here.

JORDAN: Oh my gracious. Oh my gracious. How does she look?

NICK: Beautiful.

JORDAN: Obviously.

NICK: Glowing.

JORDAN: Happy? Oh, does she look happy?

NICK: Yes.

JORDAN: She's going to find out I had a hand in this. She isn't going to hate me for it, is she?

NICK: She won't.

(Beat)

JORDAN: We should probably talk about us or something. About what happened.

NICK: I'm glad, I mean—

JORDAN: I'm glad, too.

(Beat)

NICK: He's dressed in a—

JORDAN: Yes! Yes! Tell me what they're wearing.

NICK: He's in a white suit, silver shirt, gold tie.

JORDAN: Cloth of gold. Oh my heart.

NICK: He was so…you were right. He's afraid.

JORDAN: Can you hear anything?

NICK: Nothing. Silence.

JORDAN: What's she wearing?

NICK: I don't remember.

JORDAN: Oh come on.

NICK: Lavender hat.

JORDAN: I know that hat. Oh, that's a good hat.

(GATSBY *and* DAISY, *holding hands, join* NICK. DAISY *has been crying, but she is smiling now.)*

JORDAN: Do you think they might be—

*(*NICK *hangs up violently in the middle of* JORDAN*'s last word.)*

GATSBY: Hello, old sport.

NICK: It's stopped raining.

GATSBY: Has it? What do you think of that? It's stopped raining.

DAISY: I'm glad, Jay.

GATSBY: I want you and Daisy to come over to my house. I'd like to show her around.

NICK: You're sure you want me to come?

GATSBY: Absolutely, old sport.

(During the following, the screens fill with images from the kind of brochure a realtor would create to market a very high-end property, or the tour booklet for a great house-turned-museum.)

(In the previous scene at GATSBY*'s place, we have only been on the grounds. Now we are entering the house itself.)*

(As the scene goes on, the screens become a rapidly shifting catalogue of luxury consumer goods towering over the characters.)

(The CREW *rapidly roll out a succession of rugs, each atop the last. The only practical furniture and props appear—just in time—when they get to* GATSBY*'s simple and functional private apartment. It's as if the* CREW *has an investment in enabling* GATSBY*'s display of success.)*

*(*GATSBY*'s place is an incoherent repository of the artifacts of many times and places. In its excess, it's a monument to the past so frenetic as to become a vision of the future. A kind of*

surrealist collage. Wild, impossible juxtapositions. Interiors by Max Ernst. The drive of acquisition ending in chaos.)

GATSBY: My house looks well, doesn't it? See how the whole front of it catches the light.

NICK: It's splendid.

GATSBY: Yes. It took me just three years to earn the money that bought it.

NICK: I thought you inherited your money.

GATSBY: I did, old sport, but I lost most of it in the big panic—the panic of the war.

NICK: What business are you in?

GATSBY: *(Sharply)* That's my affair. *(Righting himself)* I've been in several things. I was in the drugstore business and then I was in the oil business. But I'm not in either one now. Have you been thinking over what I proposed the other night?

DAISY: This whole huge place is yours?

GATSBY: Do you like it?

DAISY: I love it, but I don't see how you live there all alone.

GATSBY: I keep it always full of interesting people, night and day. People who do interesting things. Celebrated people. *(Calling)* Who's here?

DAISY: The gardens. The sparkling odor of jonquils. The frothy odor of hawthorn and plum blossoms. The pale gold odor of kiss-me-at-the-gate. The bird voices in the trees.

*(*KLIPSPRINGER *enters, in pajamas.)*

KLIPSPRINGER: Sorry. Got lost trying to find you.

GATSBY: Maestro Ewing Klipspringer, everyone. Were you asleep, old sport?

KLIPSPRINGER: I was doing my liver exercises.

GATSBY: I know what we'll do, we'll have Klipspringer play the piano. Ewing?

KLIPSPRINGER: I'm not warmed up. I don't—I'm all out of—Fine. *(He exits. Beat. Off)* I'm all out of practice, you see. I don't know if I can—

GATSBY: Don't talk so much, old sport! Play!

(From a little distance, a languid suite for solo piano of some romantic popular tunes of the day: The Love Nest, The Sheik of Araby.*)*

(Projections form a synthetic cubist collage illustrating GATSBY's *guided tour of his possessions.)*

GATSBY: Marie Antoinette's music room. A Restoration salon. The Merton College Library. Period bedrooms.

DAISY: Rose and lavender silk and vivid with new flowers.

GATSBY: Dressing rooms, poolrooms, bathrooms with sunken baths—and my own apartment, a bedroom, bath, an Adam study. Sit. Glass of Chartreuse?

(Bottle and glasses appear. GATSBY *starts to pour.)*

*(*DAISY *picks up* GATSBY's *hairbrush and looks at it.)*

DAISY: Gold…

*(*DAISY *brushes her hair with* GATSBY's *gold-backed hairbrush.)*

*(*GATSBY *watches this and is overwhelmed, as will happen to a person whose dream is coming true before their very eyes.)*

GATSBY: It's the funniest thing, old sport, I can't— When I try to— *(Not quite in his right mind)* I've got a man in England who buys me clothes. He sends over a selection of things at the beginning of each season, spring and fall. *(He throws shirts before them.)* Sheer linen, thick silk, fine flannel, stripes and scrolls and plaids in coral and apple-green and lavender and faint orange, and monograms of Indian blue.

(DAISY, *likewise beside herself, bends her head into the shirts and begins to cry stormily.*)

DAISY: They're such beautiful shirts. It makes me sad because I've never seen such—such beautiful shirts before.

GATSBY: I want you to see the grounds and the swimming pool, and the hydroplane and the midsummer flowers—

(NICK *is from Saint Paul, Minnesota, and it turns out there is only so much ecstasy he is prepared to bear.*)

NICK: It's begun to rain again.

GATSBY: If it wasn't for the mist, we could see your home across the bay. You have a green light that burns all night at the end of your dock.

NICK: Who's this in this picture with you?

GATSBY: That? That's Mr Dan Cody, old sport.

NICK: The name sounds faintly familiar.

GATSBY: He's dead now. He used to be my best friend years ago.

DAISY: I adore it! Your pompadour! You never told me you had a pompadour—or a yacht.

GATSBY: Look at this. Here's a lot of clippings—about you.

(*A phone rings.* GATSBY *picks it up.*)

GATSBY: Yes... Well, I can't talk now...I can't talk now, old sport...I said a small town... He must know what a small town is.... Well, he's no use to us if Detroit is his idea of a small town...

DAISY: Come here quick! Look at that. I'd like to just get one of those pink clouds and put you in it and push you around.

NICK: I should go.

GATSBY: No, old sport.

DAISY: We wouldn't hear of it.

(And so NICK *finds himself trapped in the House of Love.)*

KLIPSPRINGER: *(Singing, off)*
In the morning,
In the evening,
Ain't we got fun!
One thing's sure and nothing's surer
The rich get richer and the poor get—children!
In the meantime,
In between time,
Ain't we got fun!

(The lights fade.)

Scene 6:
Party at Gatsby's

(By now, the scale of GATSBY's *ambition is too vast to be confined to the stage alone and must break right through the fourth wall. Everyone is welcome at this party. From the lip of the stage,* GATSBY *greets and introduces people in the audience, seemingly by name. His handful of invited guests—*DAISY, TOM, *and* NICK—*stand nearby and speculate.)*

GATSBY: *(To the audience)* I'm delighted to see you! I'm delighted that you dropped in! Have a cigarette or a cigar! I'll have something to drink for you in just a minute!

DAISY: These things excite me so. If you want to kiss me any time during the evening, Nick, just let me know and I'll be glad to arrange it for you. Just mention my name. Or present a green card. I'm giving out green—

GATSBY: Look around.

DAISY: I'm looking around. I'm having a marvelous—

GATSBY: You must see the faces of many people you've heard about. *(Starting to point out people in the audience)* Perhaps you know that lady from the motion pictures.

DAISY: She's lovely.

GATSBY: The man leaning over her is her director. And Newton Orchid, who controls Films Par Excellence, and Eckhaust and Clyde Cohen and Don S Schwartze—the son—and Arthur McCarty, they're all connected with the movies in one way or another.

NICK: Aren't there any theater people? Ah there! Gus Waize and Horace O'Donavan—

GATSBY: Lester Meyer, George Duckweed, Francis Bull—

TOM: Is it all show people? We don't go around very much. I don't know a soul here.

GATSBY: Easily remedied. Everyone! This is Mrs. Buchanan...and Mr. Buchanan—the polo player.

TOM: Oh no, not me.

DAISY: I've never met so many celebrities!

NICK: Is Benny McClenahan here?

GATSBY: Haven't seen him—

NICK: Benny McClenahan always arrives with four girls.

DAISY: Tom! Your new best friend!

NICK: They're never quite the same ones, but they're so identical that it seems you've seen them before. I forget their names—

(As NICK *speaks to* DAISY, GATSBY *speaks to* TOM.*)*

GATSBY: I believe we've met somewhere before, Mr Buchanan.

TOM: Oh, yes, so we did. I remember very well.

NICK: Jaqueline, I think, or else Consuela, or Gloria or Judy or June—

GATSBY: About two weeks ago.

TOM: That's right. You were with Nick here.

NICK: And their last names are either the melodious names of flowers and months—

GATSBY: I know your wife.

*(*NICK *falls silent.)*

TOM: That so? You live near here, Nick?

NICK: Next door.

TOM: Listen, though. I'd a little rather not be the polo player. I'd rather look at all these famous people in—in oblivion.

GATSBY: Plenty of your neighbors here, as well, Buchanan. Excellent chance to meet them.

TOM: East Egg people, here?

GATSBY: From East Egg… *(Peering outward again)* The Chester Beckers and the Leeches—

NICK: There's Bunsen! Hey, Bunsen!

TOM: Good heavens, we knew him at Yale.

GATSBY: And the Hornbeams and the Willie Voltaires—

DAISY: Tom! It's the Ismays, from the club! And are those the Chrysties?

GATSBY: Those are actually Hubert Auerbach and Mr Chrystie's wife. And Edgar Beaver, whose hair turned cotton-white last weekend for no good reason at all. Clarence Endive, he got in a fistfight with…S B Whitebait, there he is, they seem to have made up.

NICK: Maurice A Flink, and the Hammerheads. The Ripley Snells! I thought—

GATSBY: Snell is due to report to the penitentiary three days from now. Securities fraud. There's old Gulick!

TOM: Senator Gulick?

GATSBY: G Earl Muldoon…

TOM: He was in the papers, he strangled his wife!

GATSBY: No, that was his brother. Though he's here, too… There's Jewett—head of the American Legion. Do you enjoy games of chance, Mr Buchanan?

DAISY: Famous risk-taker, our Tom.

GATSBY: Some of our West Egg neighbors have a little card game, Da Fontano the promoter, Ed Legros, James B Ferret—Rot-Gut Ferret—they're all here to gamble, and here's a little stock tip: if later tonight old Rot-Gut Ferret wanders into the garden, it means he was cleaned out and tomorrow morning some Class-A Associated Traction securities will be going on the market for a song.

(A REPORTER *sidles up.*)

REPORTER: Mr Gatsby? I'm with the Morning Tribune.

GATSBY: Excuse me. Yes?

TOM: Do you mind if I go talk with some people over here? A fellow looks like he's getting off some funny stuff.

DAISY: Go ahead, and if you want to take down any addresses here's my little gold pencil.

(TOM *exits.*)

REPORTER: Do you have anything to say?

GATSBY: Anything to say about what?

NICK: What's Tom up to?

DAISY: He's talking to a girl. She's common, of course. But she's pretty. I need some air.

(NICK *and* DAISY *cross away.*)

REPORTER: Why—any statement to give out. Your name has been getting around.

GATSBY: In what connection?

REPORTER: In connection with an underground pipeline to Canada.

GATSBY: You got me. I'm planning to corner the market in maple syrup.

REPORTER: There's a story that you don't live in this house, that you don't live in a house at all, that you live in a boat that looks like a house and moves by night up and down the Long Island shore.

GATSBY: Does this place look like, what, some sort of Mississippi riverboat?

REPORTER: As a matter of fact, it does, a bit.

GATSBY: That's marvelous, old sport. Have a drink, have anything you want, and go searching for the steam engine and the paddle wheels. Let me know if they turn up.

REPORTER: If I find a champagne bottle, can I break it over the bow?

GATSBY: Absolutely! Launch us all into Long Island Sound!

(*They share a laugh. The* REPORTER *heads off, satisfied for now.*)

(Meanwhile, DAISY and NICK find themselves accosted by three extremely loudly intoxicated people.)

MISS HAAG: Mrs. Buchanan! I thought it was you!

DAISY: Why, Miss Haag!

MISS HAAG: Come play golf with me at the club tomorrow!

(MISS BAEDEKER suddenly lets out a short, piercing scream. DAISY gives an alarmed little shriek in response. The others take it in stride.)

NICK: How do you feel, Miss Baedeker?

MISS BAEDEKER: Wha'?

MISS HAAG: Oh, she's all right now. When she's had five or six cocktails she always starts screaming like that. I tell her she ought to leave it alone.

MISS BAEDEKER: I do leave it alone.

MISS HAAG: We heard you yelling, so I said to Doc Civet here: "There's somebody that needs your help, Doc."

DR CIVET: She's much obliged, I'm sure, but you got her dress all wet when you stuck her head in the pool.

MISS BAEDEKER: Anything I hate is to get my head stuck in a pool. They almost drowned me once over in New Jersey.

DR CIVET: Then you ought to leave it alone.

MISS BAEDEKER: Speak for yourself! Your hand shakes, Doctor. I wouldn't let you operate on me!

(As they stagger off:)

MISS HAAG: Golf, Mrs Buchanan! It's a date!

(They are gone.)

(MISS BAEDEKER screams again.)

NICK: You're not having a good time.

DAISY: When I'm with him.

NICK: Here he comes—oops, no.

(GATSBY, *trying to reach* DAISY, *is waylaid by* SLOANE.)

SLOANE: Mr Gatsby, I had hoped to speak with you about Walter Chase.

GATSBY: Welcome to my home. Get you anything?

SLOANE: Walter Chase is my business partner. Sloane.

GATSBY: Mr Sloane, yes, I know the name.

SLOANE: Mr Chase is—

GATSBY: Mr Chase has gotten in over his head.

SLOANE: He is a friend as well as my—

GATSBY: There's nothing I can do. Get you anything at all? Champagne? Lemonade?

SLOANE: I ought to be starting home.

GATSBY: Please don't hurry off. Mingle. I'm sure you'll find people you know.

(*The music swells.*)

(DAISY *waits with* NICK, *watching* GATSBY.)

GATSBY: And now if you'll excuse me.

(DAISY *and* GATSBY *move toward each other.*)

(SLOANE *goes.*)

GATSBY: May I?

(DAISY *and* GATSBY *dance, surprisingly, a graceful, conservative foxtrot.*)

(NICK *watches.*)

(TOM *appears at* NICK'*s side.*)

TOM: I don't know a soul there. I wonder where in the devil he met Daisy. By God, I may be old-fashioned in my ideas, but women run around too much these days to suit me. They meet all kinds of crazy fish.

NICK: Literally standing with that girl's address in your pocket.

TOM: Who is this Gatsby anyhow? Some big bootlegger?

NICK: Where'd you hear that?

TOM: A lot of these newly rich people are just big bootleggers, you know. These people—

NICK: Not Gatsby.

TOM: I'd like to know who he is and what he does, and I think I'll make a point of finding out.

NICK: I've heard he owned some drugstores, a lot of drugstores. He built them up himself.

(The dance ends. DAISY and GATSBY join NICK and TOM.)

TOM: You looked like you were having fun.

DAISY: In fact we were having a bit of a row.

TOM: That so. What about?

DAISY: I can't remember now. *(Doing her TOM voice)* The future of the Nordic race.

TOM: Well, Gatsby, you certainly must have strained yourself to get this menagerie together.

DAISY: Lots of people come who haven't been invited. At least they're more interesting than the people we know.

TOM: You didn't look so interested.

NICK: You looked pretty interested when that girl started screaming.

DAISY: That girl hadn't been invited. They simply force their way in and Mr Gatsby here is too polite to object. Thank you, Mr Gatsby, for a lovely evening.

TOM: Good night.

(GATSBY *nods formally.*)

DAISY: Good night, Nick.

(TOM *and* DAISY *exit.*)

GATSBY: She didn't like it.

NICK: Of course she did.

GATSBY: She didn't like it. She didn't have a good time. I feel far away from her. It's hard to make her understand.

NICK: You mean about the party?

GATSBY: The party is unimportant. The parties are done, they've served their purpose.

NICK: Are you going away?

GATSBY: No, old sport.

NICK: Did you fire all your servants? Tonight I didn't recognize—

GATSBY: I wanted people who wouldn't gossip. Daisy comes over quite often in the afternoons. They're some people Wolfsheim wanted to do something for.

NICK: I see.

GATSBY: That thing she said. About the Nordic race.

NICK: That's her husband. It's the kind of thing he talks about a lot these days.

GATSBY: She was thinking about him. Of course she was. She's going to leave him.

NICK: She said so?

GATSBY: She says it's just a matter of time. She'll go to him and say: "I never loved you". When she does that, the last five years will disappear. We'll go back to Louisville and be married from her house—as if it were five years ago. My life has been—confused since then, but if she does that, I can fix it. She'll understand. She understood me then. We'd sit for hours…

NICK: I wouldn't ask too much of her. You can't repeat the past.

GATSBY: Can't repeat the past? Why of course you can!

(GATSBY *exits.* NICK *watches him go.*)

(NICK *starts to exit as the* CREW *comes on to change the scene.*)

(NICK *pauses for a moment to watch one of the* MEN. *Loneliness*)

(*The* MAN *sees him and nods.* NICK *smiles shily.*)

(*The* MAN *takes a step in* NICK's *direction.*)

(NICK *turns, frightened, lowers his head and walks away.*)

Scene 7:
Drinks with the Buchanans

(*Back at the Buchanan's, as in Scene 1.*)

(DAISY *and* JORDAN *are prostrate on the sofa.*)

(*The* MAID *admits* NICK *and* GATSBY.)

(GATSBY *is dressed, as he thinks, for the occasion, in a pink suit.*)

DAISY & JORDAN: We can't move.

NICK: And Mr Thomas Buchanan, the athlete?

JORDAN: The rumor is that that's Tom's girl on the telephone.

TOM: (*Off*) Very well, then, I won't sell you the car at all…I'm under no obligations to you at all…and as for your bothering me about it at lunch time, I won't stand that at all!

DAISY: Holding down the receiver.

NICK: No, he's not. It's a bona-fide deal. I happen to know about it.

(TOM *enters.*)

TOM: Mr Gatsby! I'm glad to see you, sir…Nick…

DAISY: Make us a cold drink.

(TOM *exits.* DAISY *kisses* GATSBY *on the mouth.*)

DAISY: You know I love you.

JORDAN: You forget there's a lady present.

DAISY: You kiss Nick too.

JORDAN: *(Being her aunt)* What a low, vulgar girl!

DAISY: I don't care!

(TOM *enters, preceding four gin rickeys that click full of ice.*)

GATSBY: They certainly look cool.

TOM: I read somewhere that the sun's getting hotter every year. It seems that pretty soon the earth's going to fall into the sun—or wait a minute—it's just the opposite—the sun's getting colder every year. Come outside. I'd like you to have a look at the place.

GATSBY: I'm right across the water from you.

TOM: So you are.

DAISY: What'll we do with ourselves this afternoon? And the day after that, and the next thirty years?

JORDAN: Don't be morbid. Life starts all over again when it gets crisp in the fall.

DAISY: But it's so hot, and everything's so confused. Let's all go to town!

TOM: I've heard of making a garage out of a stable, but I'm the first man who ever made a stable out of a garage.

DAISY: Who wants to go to town? Ah, you look so cool. You always look so cool. You resemble the advertisement of the man… You know the advertisement of the man…

(DAISY *is looking at* GATSBY *as if he were the only man in the room, or maybe the world. Even* TOM *can see it.*)

JORDAN: Those big movies around Fiftieth Street are cool. I love New York on summer afternoons when every one's away. There's something very sensuous about it—overripe, as if all sorts of funny fruits were going to fall into your hands.

DAISY: Where are we going?

JORDAN: How about the movies?

DAISY: It's so hot. You go. We'll ride around and meet you after. We'll meet you on some corner. I'll be the man smoking two cigarettes.

TOM: We can't argue about it here. We'll take two cars and meet on the south side of Central Park, in front of the Plaza.

DAISY: Let's get a suite in the Plaza. We'll hire five bathrooms and take cold baths.

TOM: That's a crazy idea.

JORDAN: It'll be a place to have a mint julep.

NICK: It is a crazy idea.

TOM: All right, I'm perfectly willing to go to town. Come on—we're all going to town. Come on! What's the matter, anyhow?

DAISY: Are we just going to go? Like this?

TOM: If we're going to town, let's start.

DAISY: Have it your own way. Come on, Jordan.

(DAISY *and* JORDAN *exit. An awkward moment*)

GATSBY: So you've got your stables here?

TOM: About a quarter of a mile down the road. I don't see the idea of going to town. Women get these notions in their heads—

DAISY: *(Off)* Shall we take anything to drink?

TOM: I'll get some whiskey. *(He exits.)*

NICK: I was afraid the two of you would make some kind of scene.

GATSBY: I can't say anything in his house, old sport.

NICK: She's got an indiscreet voice. It's full of...

GATSBY: Her voice is full of money.

NICK: That's it. I never understood before. It's full of money.

GATSBY: She's a king's daughter, high in a white palace, the golden girl...

(TOM, DAISY, and JORDAN enter.)

GATSBY: Shall we all go in my car?

TOM: Is it standard shift?

GATSBY: Yes.

TOM: Well, you take my coupe and let me drive your car to town.

GATSBY: I don't think there's much gas.

TOM: Plenty of gas. And if it runs out I can stop at a drugstore. You can buy anything at a drugstore nowadays. Come on, Daisy, I'll take you in his circus wagon.

DAISY: You take Nick and Jordan. We'll follow you in the coupe.

(GATSBY and DAISY exit.)

(Engines. Billboards and projections)

(TOM, NICK, and JORDAN stand close together as the CREW works to transform the space twice in rapid succession, first taking it down to the grey of the Valley of Ashes.)

TOM: Did you see that!

NICK: See what?

TOM: You think I'm pretty dumb, don't you! Perhaps I am, but I have a—almost a second sight, sometimes, that tells me what to do. Maybe you don't believe that, but science—I've made a small investigation of this fellow.

JORDAN: And you found out he was an Oxford man.

TOM: An Oxford man! Like hell he is! He wears a pink suit!

JORDAN: Nevertheless he's an Oxford man.

TOM: Oxford, New Mexico, or something like that.

JORDAN: Listen, Tom. If you're such a snob, why did you invite him to lunch?

TOM: Daisy invited him; she knew him before we were married—God knows where!

NICK: Gasoline.

TOM: We've got enough to get us to town.

JORDAN: But there's a garage right here. I don't want to get stalled in this baking heat.

(Engine dies, lights and projections change to gas station signage.)

(Horn honking. NICK and JORDAN wander while TOM shouts:)

TOM: Let's have some gas! What do you think we stopped for—to admire the view? Wilson!

(GEORGE enters.)

TOM: There you are! What's the matter with you?

GEORGE: Hi, Mr Buchanan. I'm sick. Been sick all day.

TOM: What's the matter?

MYRTLE: *(Off)* Get back up here, you bastard!

GEORGE: I'm all run down.

TOM: Well, shall I help myself? You sounded well enough on the phone.

GEORGE: I didn't mean to interrupt your lunch. But I need money pretty bad, and I was wondering what you were going to do with your old car.

TOM: *(Pointing off)* How do you like the one I'm driving?

GEORGE: It's a nice yellow one.

TOM: Like to buy it?

GEORGE: Big chance. No, but I could make some money on the other.

TOM: What do you want money for, all of a sudden?

GEORGE: I've been here too long. I want to get away.

MYRTLE: *(Off)* Unlock the Goddamn door!

GEORGE: My wife and I want to go West.

TOM: Your wife does?

GEORGE: She's been talking about it for ten years, now she's going whether she wants to or not. I'm going to get her away.

TOM: What do I owe you?

MYRTLE: *(Off)* Get up here, you dirty little coward!

GEORGE: Sorry. I've got her locked in up there.

MYRTLE: *(Off)* Beat me! Throw me down and beat me, you dirty little coward!

GEORGE: *(Shouting upward)* You're going to stay there till the day after tomorrow, and then we're going to move away!

TOM: What happened?

GEORGE: I just got wised up to something funny the last two days. There's times she disappears. To see her sister she says. But now I've been thinking about those times. So I thought maybe I should ask you.

(Beat)

TOM: Ask me what?

GEORGE: About that car. I want to get us away. That's why I been bothering you about the car.

MYRTLE: *(Off)* Hey!

TOM: What do I owe you?

GEORGE: Dollar twenty.

TOM: I'll let you have that car. I'll send it over tomorrow afternoon.

MYRTLE: *(Off)* You rotten son of a bitch!

(GEORGE exits as the lights and projections change:)

(A suite at the Plaza Hotel. Conspicuously empty of furniture for a moment, but a rug has appeared and the light is good.)

(Somewhere close by, the sounds of a wedding, which continue.)

(As the party make themselves as comfortable as they can, the CREW finishes assembling the suite around them.)

JORDAN: It's a swell suite.

DAISY: Open another window.

JORDAN: There aren't any more.

DAISY: Well, we'd better telephone for an ax—

TOM: The thing to do is to forget about the heat. You make it ten times worse by crabbing about it.

GATSBY: Why not let her alone, old sport? You're the one that wanted to come to town.

TOM: That's a great expression of yours, isn't it?

GATSBY: What is?

TOM: All this "old sport" business. Where'd you pick that up?

DAISY: Now see here, Tom, if you're going to make personal remarks I won't stay here a minute. Call up and order some ice for the mint juleps.

(TOM *picks up the receiver.*)

(*Mendelssohn's* Wedding March *from the ballroom below.*)

JORDAN: Imagine marrying anybody in this heat!

DAISY: I was married in the middle of June. Louisville in June! Somebody fainted. Who was it fainted, Tom?

TOM: Biloxi.

DAISY: A man named Biloxi. "Blocks" Biloxi, and he made boxes—that's a fact—and he was from Biloxi, Tennessee.

JORDAN: They carried him into my house, because we lived just two doors from the church. And he stayed three weeks, until Daddy told him he had to get out. The day after he left Daddy died. There wasn't any connection.

NICK: I used to know a Bill Biloxi from Memphis.

JORDAN: That was his cousin. I knew his whole family history before he left. He gave me an aluminum putter that I still use today.

(*The music had died down as the ceremony began and now a long cheer floats in, followed by intermittent cries of "Yea-ea-ea!" and finally by a burst of jazz as the dancing begins.*)

DAISY: We're getting old. If we were young, we'd rise and dance.

JORDAN: Remember Biloxi? Where'd you know him, Tom?

TOM: Biloxi? I didn't know him. He was a friend of Daisy's.

DAISY: He was not. I'd never seen him before. He came down in the private rail car with you.

TOM: Well, he said he knew you. He said he was raised in Louisville. Asa Bird brought him around at the last minute and asked if we had room for him.

JORDAN: He was probably bumming his way home. He told me he was president of your class at Yale.

NICK: Biloxi?

TOM: First place, we didn't have any president—

(GATSBY's foot is beating a short, restless tattoo.)

Tom: By the way, Mr Gatsby, I understand you're an Oxford man.

GATSBY: Not exactly.

TOM: Oh, yes, I understand you went to Oxford.

GATSBY: Yes—I went there.

(A knock)

TOM: You must have gone there about the time Biloxi went to Yale.

(Since no one else is moving, NICK goes out, and returns with crushed mint and ice.)

GATSBY: I told you I went there.

TOM: I heard you, but I'd like to know when.

GATSBY: It was in 1919. I stayed only five months. That's why I can't really call myself an Oxford man. It was an opportunity they gave to some of the

officers after the Armistice. We could go to any of the
universities in England or France.

DAISY: Open the whiskey, Tom, and I'll make you
a mint julep. Then you won't seem so stupid to
yourself... Look at the mint!

TOM: I've made a little investigation into your affairs,
Mr. Gatsby.

GATSBY: You can suit yourself about that, old sport.

TOM: Who is Dan Cody?

GATSBY: Dan Cody was my best friend, before the war.
Famous in his day.

TOM: Some kind of robber baron out of the West?
Brothels and gold mines?

GATSBY: He was old by then. Living on a magnificent
sailboat. He saw something in me. You're always
grateful to someone who does that. He took me on as
crew and we traveled the world. I know my manners
can seem old fashioned, but they're the ways I learned
from him.

(Beat)

DAISY: So the old wealthy family? Generations at
Oxford?

GATSBY: When I speak of my family, I am thinking of
him. He made me what I am. And the war did. And
you did. You saw something in me, too. You believed
I was the man I had always imagined I was. Now I am
that man. Whatever we said then, it's true now. It just
took me some time.

TOM: One thing I can't find out is your real name.
There's no record of your ever being born.

GATSBY: My name is Jay Gatsby. Everybody knows
that.

TOM: And what are you, anyway?

(Beat)

NICK: He's a war hero, Tom. And a self-made man.

TOM: See, right there. People like you think that what matters about a man is what he's done. People like us—tell him, Daisy—our kind of people only care about what a man is. Who his people are. Nothing good a man like you can do makes a damn bit of difference, and the crimes just reveal the kind of shithole you're from.

DAISY: Tom!

GATSBY: Mr Buchanan, I hear you were very tough on the football field as a college boy. I hear you're very tough with women.

TOM: I'm not some street-corner thug, if that's what you're getting at.

DAISY: Jay. Let's just go.

GATSBY: All right. Then I believe we will take our leave.

TOM: Wait a minute. I want to ask Mr Gatsby one more question.

GATSBY: Go on.

TOM: What kind of a row are you trying to cause in my house anyhow?

DAISY: He isn't causing a row. You're causing a row. Please have a little self-control.

TOM: Self-control! I suppose the latest thing is to sit back and let Mr Nobody from Nowhere make love to your wife. Well, if that's the idea you can count me out. Nowadays people begin by sneering at family life and family institutions, and next they'll throw everything overboard and have intermarriage between black and white.

JORDAN: We're all white here.

TOM: I know I'm not very popular. I don't give big parties. I suppose you've got to make your house into a pigsty in order to have any friends—in the modern world.

GATSBY: I've got something to tell you, old sport—

DAISY: Please don't! Please let's all go home. Why don't we all go home?

NICK: That's a good idea. Come on, Tom. Nobody wants a drink.

TOM: I want to know what Mr Gatsby has to tell me.

GATSBY: Your wife doesn't love you. She's never loved you. She loves me.

TOM: You must be crazy!

GATSBY: She never loved you, do you hear? She only married you because I was poor and she was tired of waiting for me. It was a terrible mistake, but in her heart she never loved anyone but me!

NICK: Let's go.

JORDAN: Let's.

TOM & GATSBY: No!

TOM: Stay right there, Daisy. What's been going on? I want to hear all about it.

GATSBY: I told you what's been going on, going on for five years—and you didn't know.

TOM: You've been seeing this fellow for five years?

GATSBY: Not seeing. No, we couldn't meet. But both of us loved each other all that time, old sport, and you didn't know. I used to laugh sometimes to think that you didn't know.

TOM: Oh—that's all. You're crazy! I can't speak about what happened five years ago, because I didn't know Daisy then—and I'll be damned if I see how you got within a mile of her unless you brought the groceries to the back door. But all the rest of that's a God damned lie. Daisy loved me when she married me and she loves me now.

GATSBY: No.

TOM: She does, though. The trouble is that sometimes she gets foolish ideas in her head and doesn't know what she's doing. And what's more, I love Daisy too. Once in a while I go off on a spree and make a fool of myself, but I always come back, and in my heart I love her all the time.

DAISY: You're revolting. Do you know why we left Chicago? I guess nobody's heard the story of that little spree.

GATSBY: Daisy, that's all over now. It doesn't matter anymore. Just tell him the truth—that you never loved him—and it's all wiped out forever.

DAISY: Why—how could I love him—possibly?

GATSBY: You never loved him.

DAISY: I never loved him.

TOM: Not at Kapiolani?

DAISY: No.

TOM: Not that day I carried you down from the Punch Bowl to keep your shoes dry? Daisy?

DAISY: Please don't. There, Jay. Oh, you want too much! I love you now—isn't that enough? I can't help what's past. I did love him once—but I loved you too.

GATSBY: You loved me *too*?

TOM: Even that's a lie. She didn't know you were alive. Why—there're things between Daisy and me that you'll never know, things that neither of us can ever forget.

GATSBY: I want to speak to Daisy alone. She's all excited now—

DAISY: Even alone I can't say I never loved Tom. It wouldn't be true.

TOM: Of course it wouldn't.

DAISY: As if it mattered to you!

TOM: Of course it matters. I'm going to take better care of you from now on.

GATSBY: You don't understand. You're not going to take care of her anymore.

TOM: I'm not? Why's that?

GATSBY: Daisy's leaving you.

TOM: Nonsense.

DAISY: I am, though.

TOM: She's not leaving me! Certainly not for a common swindler who'd have to steal the ring he put on her finger.

DAISY: I won't stand this! Oh, please let's get out.

TOM: You're one of that bunch that hangs around with Meyer Wolfsheim. I found out what your "drugstores" were. He and this Wolfsheim bought up dozens of side-street drugstores and sold grain alcohol over the counter. I picked him for a bootlegger the first time I saw him, and I wasn't far wrong. Made his fortune selling illegal liquor.

DAISY: Literally standing with a cocktail in your hand.

GATSBY: Perfectly legal, old sport. Drug companies are exempt from the Prohibition laws.

TOM: Now you and your friends are breaking into the bond business. And all of a sudden there have started to be big robberies of bonds, and selling of forged bonds, and stolen bonds, and bucket shops selling worthless bonds, and that's not legal one bit.

GATSBY: What about it? I guess your friend Walter Chase wasn't too proud to come in with us.

TOM: And you left him in the lurch, didn't you?

GATSBY: He came to us dead broke. He was very glad to pick up some money.

TOM: You let him go to the penitentiary.

GATSBY: That was a surprise. I thought men of his breeding usually shot themselves before they would submit to the disgrace, old sport.

TOM: Don't you call me "old sport"! Walter could have testified against you, but Wolfsheim scared him into shutting his mouth, didn't he? People like you and Wolfsheim—nobody can touch you. Hoodlums. Gunsels. Gangsters!

(GATSBY *gets a look on his face and in his body that no one else in this room has ever seen in their lives, and everyone suddenly remembers that they have heard that he has killed a man. Now they believe it.*)

DAISY: Jay! Don't hurt him!

(GATSBY *has barely moved. But they have all seen, and that is enough.*)

DAISY: Please, Tom! I can't stand this anymore!

TOM: You two start on home, Daisy. In Mr Gatsby's car. Go on. He won't annoy you. I think he realizes that his presumptuous little flirtation is over.

(DAISY *and* GATSBY *exit.*)

TOM: Want any of this stuff? Jordan? ...Nick? Nick?

NICK: What?

TOM: Want any?

NICK: No...I just remembered. Today's my birthday. Good God. I'm thirty years old.

(The lights fade. In the dimness, the CREW clear the Plaza suite.)

(Meanwhile, engines, headlights, projections take us from Manhattan to the Valley of Ashes.)

(The automobiles crescendo.)

(Then screaming horns, screeching tires, a terrible crunching thump. Flailing headlights.)

(A moment of near silence.)

(Running feet)

(A powerful engine—we know it—roaring back to life and fading into the distance.)

(As the lights rise—moonlight, dim lights from buildings— the yellow squares of windows, and on the billboard, the spectacles.)

(In contrast to the violence of the sounds, the CREW assemble the scene with an almost reverent gentleness.)

(One lays down a patch of red.)

(MYRTLE enters, her face and torso covered in blood.)

(MICHAELIS formally offers MYRTLE a hand so that she can kneel on the patch of red.)

(GEORGE enters and stands aghast.)

(MICHAELIS leans over her.)

(New car headlights illuminate the scene.)

(TOM, NICK, and JORDAN step in, and the tableau is complete.)

Scene 8:
Hit and Run

GEORGE: Oh, my God! Oh, my God!

TOM: We'll take a look. Just a look. There's some bad trouble here.

MICHAELIS: Stay back, people!

GEORGE: Oh, my God! Oh, my God! Oh, my God! Oh, my God!

TOM: What happened here?

NICK: Has somebody called an ambulance? The police?

MICHAELIS: You, your friends keep back. She's already dead.

TOM: Are you sure? Are you sure?

MICHAELIS: It just tore her open and her mouth and the blood. She was such a lively person. And they just left her in the road.

GEORGE: Oh, my Ga-od! Oh, my Ga-od! oh, Ga-od! oh, my Ga-od!

TOM: Listen to me!

MICHAELIS: What you want, fella? Who are you?

TOM: We were driving just behind the—who are you?

MICHAELIS: Michaelis, I run the coffee joint there, by the ash heaps.

TOM: What happened?

MICHAELIS: Auto hit her. Instantly killed.

TOM: Instantly killed.

MICHAELIS: She'd been upstairs, I guess he and she been fighting. Then there's a car coming, and something breaks and Myrtle, Mrs Wilson, she's flying out the door and she's running out into the road, waving her hands and shouting—and before I could move, it was over. Son of a bitch didn't even stop his car. It came out of the dark and...drifted into her...and disappeared around the bend. She ran out there and the car coming from New York knocked right into her, going thirty or forty miles an hour.

TOM: What color was the car?

MICHAELIS: Big big car, maybe green, light green—

TOM: Listen. Could it have been a yellow car?

MICHAELIS: It could have been a yellow car, big yellow car. New. Did you see it?

TOM: It passed me down the road, going faster than forty. Going fifty, sixty.

GEORGE: You don't have to tell me what kind of car it was! I know what kind of car it was!

TOM: You've got to pull yourself together. Listen, listen, I just got here a minute ago, from New York. I was bringing you that coupe we've been talking about. That yellow car I was driving this afternoon wasn't mine—do you hear? I haven't seen it all afternoon.

MICHAELIS: What's all this?

TOM: I'm a friend of his. If you know the car that did it... It was a yellow car.

MICHAELIS: And what color's your car?

TOM: My car is a blue car, a blue coupe, right over there.

NICK: We've come straight from New York.

TOM: Wilson! You've seen that yellow car before. Yes? Yes? You know who owns that car.

NICK: Tom.

TOM: The owner of that car is a Mister Jay Gatsby.

NICK: Tom, we should wait for the police.

TOM: Mister Jay Gatsby, who lives in that big, big house, that mansion, with all the lights, where they have all the parties. In West Egg. He's a powerful man, a wealthy man. If the police could do anything to touch Mister Jay Gatsby, they would have done it by now. Mister Jay Gatsby is above the laws of man and God. Nick, Jordan. Let's get out.

NICK: Shouldn't we wait for the police?

TOM: The Goddamned coward! He didn't even stop his car.

(TOM *strides out, with* NICK *and* JORDAN *close behind.*)

(GEORGE *and* MICHAELIS *are left behind, by the kneeling body of* MYRTLE.)

(*Distant sirens*)

GEORGE: He murdered her.

MICHAELIS: It was an accident, George. You don't know what you're saying. Try and sit quiet.

GEORGE: I know I'm one of these trusting fellas and I don't think any harm to nobody, but when I get to know a thing I know it. It was the man in that car. She ran out to speak to him and he wouldn't stop.

MICHAELIS: I saw it, too, but I didn't put any significance on it. I thought she was…well, I thought you two were fighting and she was trying to get away. How could she of been like that?

GEORGE: She's a deep one. Ah God. Ah-h-h God.

(*The lights fade.*)

(*The* CREW *disassembles the death scene.*)

Scene 9:
Vigil

(East Egg, outside the BUCHANAN's, *night.)*

*(*TOM, JORDAN, *and* NICK*)*

TOM: Lights are on. Daisy's home. There's nothing we can do tonight. Come in.

NICK: No. I'll find my own way home.

*(*TOM *exits.)*

JORDAN: Won't you come in, Nick?

NICK: No, thanks.

JORDAN: It's only half-past nine.

NICK: Haven't you had enough of them for one day?

*(*JORDAN *turns abruptly and runs off.)*

*(*NICK *stands for a moment with his head in his hands.)*

*(*GATSBY *enters and watches him.)*

GATSBY: Evening, old sport.

NICK: What are you doing?

GATSBY: Just standing here.

NICK: Alone?

GATSBY: Did you see any trouble on the road?

NICK: Yes.

GATSBY: Was she killed?

NICK: Yes.

GATSBY: I thought so; I told Daisy I thought so. It's better that the shock should all come at once. She stood it pretty well. I got to West Egg by a side road and left the car in my garage. I don't think anybody saw us, but of course I can't be sure. Did anyone see us, do you know?

NICK: How would I know?

GATSBY: Who was the woman?

(Lights up on another area: the Valley of Ashes, Wilson's Garage.)

(GEORGE and MICHAELIS sit, benumbed.)

NICK: Her name was Myrtle Wilson. Her husband owns the garage. How the devil did it happen?

GATSBY: Well, I tried to swing the wheel—

NICK: Was Daisy driving?

GATSBY: Yes. But of course I'll say I was. When we left New York she was very nervous and she thought it would steady her to drive—and this woman rushed out at us—

(Lights up on JORDAN and DAISY, inside the BUCHANAN's.)

DAISY: I never saw her!

(So now in three separate areas of light, there are three pairs: NICK and GATSBY, GEORGE and MICHAELIS, JORDAN and DAISY.)

(DAISY is pacing relentlessly across and back, much as she did in JORDAN's tour of her history in Scene 4, but now she's trapped in the same moment over and over. JORDAN watches from the sofa.)

DAISY: Another car swerved and I swerved and they must have been swerving around her because I missed that car but there was a bump, it pushed our car and I tried to steer but he had grabbed the wheel and I couldn't do anything and by then we were past them.

JORDAN: You didn't go back.

DAISY: I didn't know what happened it was just a noise, I didn't know what it was.

JORDAN: You didn't see her?

DAISY: I didn't see anything I never saw anything.

JORDAN: Tom will fix it.

DAISY: No. No.

JORDAN: Is there a plan? Does somebody have a plan?

DAISY: I'm a good driver, I'm not a bad driver, you're a bad driver, this kind of thing never happens to you. I have a perfect record and I don't see—why are you crying?

JORDAN: I saw. I saw her.

DAISY: What am I supposed to do now?

JORDAN: You could confess. You could go to the police and say you were driving.

DAISY: Tom wouldn't let me do that.

JORDAN: He couldn't really stop you.

DAISY: Is that what you would do?

(Beat)

JORDAN: Or there's Gatsby.

DAISY: You know I only get in trouble when Gatsby's around? Why does he—

JORDAN: What do you want to do?

DAISY: There's nothing to be done. We drove away.

JORDAN: Tom will fix it.

DAISY: Remember when Tom was in a car accident in Santa Barbara? And a woman was hurt? He fixed that, he paid everybody off. And me too, I guess. I should have left him then.

JORDAN: You were already pregnant.

DAISY: I will never ever ever ever ever ever—

JORDAN: Hey! I saw her! Shut up about you for one minute. She was torn open. Her breast, her mouth. The tragedy here is not you.

DAISY: Stop hurting me!

JORDAN: Jesus Christ!

(DAISY *falls into* JORDAN*'s arms, sobbing.* JORDAN *takes a moment to assess whether this is another* DAISY *performance. Then she gives in as she always does and holds her.*)

DAISY: Who was she? Does anybody know?

MICHAELIS: How long have you been married, George? Come on there, try and sit still a minute and answer my question. How long have you been married?

GEORGE: Twelve years.

MICHAELIS: Have you got a church you go to sometimes, George? Maybe even if you haven't been there for a long time? Maybe I could call up the church and get a priest to come over and he could talk to you, see?

GEORGE: Don't belong to any.

MICHAELIS: You ought to have a church, George, for times like this. You must have gone to church once. Didn't you get married in a church? Listen, George, listen to me. Didn't you get married in a church?

GEORGE: That was a long time ago. Look at this.

(GEORGE *pulls from his pocket a small, expensive dog-leash, made of leather and braided silver, apparently new. He holds it out.*)

MICHAELIS: This?

GEORGE: I found it yesterday afternoon. She had it wrapped in tissue paper on her bureau.

MICHAELIS: So she bought a dog leash. So?

GEORGE: We don't have a dog! Oh, my God! A couple
of weeks ago Myrtle came home from the city, she was
supposed to be with her sister but her face was bruised
and her nose was swollen.

MICHAELIS: What did she say happened?

GEORGE: She didn't.

MICHAELIS: But when you asked her?

GEORGE: I didn't ask her. I guess I was afraid to ask
her. Oh, my God! Then he killed her.

MICHAELIS: Who did?

GATSBY: Daisy will be all right tomorrow. I'm just
going to wait here and see if he tries to bother her
about that unpleasantness at the hotel this afternoon.
She said she would lock herself in her room.

NICK: He won't touch her. He's not thinking about her.

GATSBY: I don't trust him, old sport.

NICK: You ought to go away. It's pretty certain they'll
trace your car.

GATSBY: Go away now?

NICK: Go to Atlantic City for a week, or up to Montreal.

GATSBY: I couldn't possibly leave Daisy, not until I
know what she's going to do.

NICK: So you still…what are you hoping she'll…

GATSBY: I guess by now you know I come from
nothing. She was the first nice girl I'd ever known.
Her house amazed me. So many men wanted her.
Everything about her gleamed like silver.

JORDAN: Did you? With him? I always wondered.

DAISY: I was so curious, and he was so … determined.
He knew things about me I didn't know. And
afterward he looked at me.

JORDAN: I remember how he looked at you.

DAISY: Like I was the Holy Grail.

JORDAN: How could you … Tom Buchanan? When there was someone like that?

GATSBY: And then the war rushes you here, there, you remember, then the Armistice and I was desperate to get back to her, but instead of the States they sent me to Oxford, and by then it was too late—

DAISY: He wasn't there and everybody there was saying hurry up, hurry up, what are you waiting for, do something, pick someone, I was besieged, and I couldn't tell them, what was he, what was that, a way someone looked at you—

JORDAN: I'm not so bad and no one worthwhile has ever looked at me like that. Maybe nobody ever will. You could have had that.

DAISY: I would have lost everything else.

NICK: All this, everything you've done.

GATSBY: Years ago. Our last day before I shipped out. We just sat together.

DAISY: He held me in his arms for a long, silent time.

GATSBY: It was a cold fall day,

DAISY: With fire in the room.

GATSBY: Her cheeks flushed. Now and then she moved.

DAISY: And he would change his arm a little,

GATSBY: And once I kissed her dark, shining hair.

DAISY: I brushed my lips against the shoulder of his coat.

GATSBY: I touched the end of her fingers. Gently.

DAISY: As though I were asleep.

GATSBY: You could go a long way. You could do a lot.
To get the chance for another hour like that. And I did.
I did it, this summer. She felt it, too. She'll call.

DAISY: At least we had that hour again, this summer.
That will have to do. For this life. That will have to last
me.

JORDAN: All right then. Go to Tom, who owes you—

DAISY: I know he owns me. You don't have to—

JORDAN: He. Owes. You. He will make this go away
and you will go away. Go to him now. You're in pain.
That's how he likes you best. I would fix it for you
myself if I could.

(DAISY *slips out of* JORDAN'*s arms, collects herself, and
walks calmly out.*)

GATSBY: I don't think she ever loved him. You must
remember, old sport, she was very excited this
afternoon. He told her those things in a way that
frightened her—that made it look as if I was some kind
of cheap sharper. And the result was she hardly knew
what she was saying. Of course she might have loved
him just for a minute, when they were first married—
and loved me more even then, do you see? In any case,
it was just personal.

NICK: How long are you going to wait?

GATSBY: All night, if necessary. Anyhow, till they all go
to bed.

NICK: You wait here. I'll see if there's any sign of a
commotion.

(*In a square of yellow light, looking like an advertisement for
domestic contentment,* DAISY *and* TOM *sit together, with
a plate of cold fried chicken between them, and two bottles
of ale. He is talking intently at her, and his hand has fallen
upon and covered her own. She is looking at him, once in a*

*while nodding in agreement. They aren't happy—and yet
they aren't unhappy either. There is an unmistakable air of
natural intimacy about the picture, as if they are conspiring
together.)*

GATSBY: Is it all quiet up there?

NICK: Yes, it's all quiet. Let's better walk home and get
some sleep.

MICHAELIS: Maybe you got some friend that I could
telephone for, George?

GEORGE: I spoke to her. I told her she might fool me but
she couldn't fool God. I took her to the window and I
said "God knows what you've been doing, everything
you've been doing. You may fool me, but you can't
fool God!"

*(GEORGE points up at the billboard with the glazed eyes of
Dr. T. J. Eckleburg, pale and enormous, visible in the dawn
night.)*

GEORGE: God sees everything.

MICHAELIS: That's an advertisement.

GEORGE: Do you think God sees me?

MICHAELIS: You must close your eyes.

(GEORGE tries to close his eyes.)

*(On the projection surfaces, the covers of pulp novels
and magazines, featuring tough men with guns. On the
billboards, posters for gangster movies and westerns.
Everywhere, strong decisive action taken with a pistol.)*

(NICK and GATSBY arrive at NICK's lawn.)

(The sun will be up soon.)

(The green light is visible in the distance, the morning star.)

NICK: There it is.

GATSBY: What, old sport?

NICK: That green light.

GATSBY: Daisy's place.

NICK: I've seen you looking across at it.

GATSBY: Have you? For a long time... It's funny. It doesn't feel the same, now that I've been there.

NICK: Autumn flavor in the air.

GATSBY: You know, old sport, I've never used that swimming pool all summer? Maybe today should be the day. I'll have a telephone brought outside so I won't miss her call.

NICK: And you're sure you hadn't better try to get away?

GATSBY: I can't picture that.

NICK: You have to.

GATSBY: I can't see myself doing that. I still believe life has great things in mind for me. Look at all this. It's a dream.

NICK: Twelve minutes to my train. I have to go to work. Oh God, for Walter Chase! If there's anything left standing.

GATSBY: Call me up, old sport.

NICK: I'll call you about noon.

GATSBY: I suppose Daisy will call too?

NICK: I suppose so.

GATSBY: Well, goodbye.

(GATSBY *and* NICK *shake hands and* NICK *starts away. He turns.*)

NICK: They're a rotten crowd. You're worth the whole damn bunch put together.

(GATSBY *smiles, and goes.*)

(The phone rings. NICK *picks it up.)*

*(*JORDAN *appears, with a telephone.)*

JORDAN: You weren't so nice to me last night.

NICK: How could it have mattered then?

JORDAN: Nick, I have had a night of hell. I need to see you.

NICK: I want to see you, too.

JORDAN: Suppose I come to you this afternoon?

NICK: No—I don't think this afternoon.

JORDAN: Very well.

NICK: It's impossible this afternoon. Various—

JORDAN: Fine.

NICK: I have to make a call.

*(*NICK *hangs up. He dials.* JORDAN *dials. Busy signals.* JORDAN *dials again.)*

*(*GEORGE *enters. He has one hand in a pocket of his coverall.)*

GEORGE: Excuse me. Hello? I'm looking for Mr Gatsby's house?

NICK: Wait. I—

(The phone rings.)

NICK: What do you want? Can I help you?

GEORGE: No, no.

(The phone rings. Neither moves.)

GEORGE: You should get that.

NICK: You sure I can't—

GEORGE: *(Looking off toward* GATSBY'S*)* No, no. I see the house. Boy, you can't miss it, huh.

(The phone rings.)

(GEORGE *exits, toward* GATSBY'*s house.*)

(NICK *turns toward the phone, turns back.*)

(*A shot*)

NICK: Oh God.

(*Another shot*)

(NICK *starts running.*)

(*The lights fade.*)

Scene 10:
Memorial

(NICK *talks on the telephone, one of several around the space.*)

NICK: Mrs Buchanan, please? Mr Buchanan, then? Left no address? Did they say when they'd be back? Any idea where they are? How I could reach them? (*Hanging up, trying again*) Meyer Wolfsheim? I've rung three times. It's very important. No one's there? (*Hanging up, speaking to the air*) I'll get somebody for you, Gatsby. Don't worry. Just trust me and I'll get somebody for you—

(*A different telephone rings.* NICK *dashes to it.*)

NICK: Daisy?

(SLAGLE *enters, with a telephone.*)

(*Note: We've heard* DAISY *and* JORDAN *do pretend Chicago tough gal voices.* SLAGLE *is the genuine article.*)

SLAGLE: Chicago. This is Slagle speaking…

NICK: Yes?

SLAGLE: Hell of a note, isn't it? Get my wire?

NICK: There haven't been any wires.

SLAGLE: Young Parke's in trouble. They picked him up when he handed the bonds over the counter. They got a circular from New York giving 'em the numbers just five minutes before. What d'you know about that, hey? You never can tell in these hick towns—

NICK: Hello! Look here—this isn't Mr Gatsby. Mr. Gatsby's dead. Hello?

(NICK, having been hung up on, hangs up.)

(A different telephone rings. NICK runs to answer.)

NICK: Gatsby residence.

(KLIPSPRINGER enters, with a telephone.)

KLIPSPRINGER: Hello, who's this?

NICK: This is Mr Carraway.

KLIPSPRINGER: Oh! This is Klipspringer.

NICK: The funeral's tomorrow. Three o'clock, here at the house. I wish you'd tell anybody who'd be interested.

KLIPSPRINGER: Well, I'll certainly try. What I called up about is—

NICK: Wait a minute. How about saying you'll come?

KLIPSPRINGER: Well, the fact is—the truth of the matter is that I'm staying with some people up here in Greenwich, and they rather expect me to be with them tomorrow. In fact, there's a sort of picnic or something. Of course I'll do my very best to get away.

NICK: Huh!

KLIPSPRINGER: What I called up about was a pair of shoes I left there. You see, they're tennis shoes, and I'm sort of helpless without them. My address is care of B F—

(NICK hangs up forcefully.)

(A momentary burst of train light and sound.)

*(*NICK* is standing in an empty space, looking around confusedly.)*

NICK: Hello? Hello? Hello?

*(*WOLFSHEIM* enters.)*

NICK: Mr Wolfsheim.

WOLFSHEIM: My memory goes back to when I first met him. A young major just out of the army and covered over with medals he got in the war. He was so hard up he had to keep on wearing his uniform because he couldn't buy some regular clothes. He come into Winebrenner's poolroom at Forty-third Street and asked for a job. He hadn't eat anything for a couple of days. "Come on have some lunch with me," I said. He ate more than four dollars' worth of food in half an hour.

NICK: Did you start him in business?

WOLFSHEIM: Start him! I made him.

NICK: Oh.

WOLFSHEIM: I saw right away he was a fine-appearing, gentlemanly young man, and I knew I could use him good. And smart? Before practically everyone he saw: Prohibition, the prohibiting is what gives a thing its value. Something I guess he learned from life so young.

NICK: You were his closest friend, so I know you'll want to come to his funeral this afternoon.

WOLFSHEIM: I can't do it—I can't get mixed up in it.

NICK: There's nothing to get mixed up in. It was the act of a madman. It's all over now.

WOLFSHEIM: That may be true. Or it may have been a form of message. Like Rosy Rosenthal, if you remember we talked over that bit of history. Let us learn to show our friendship for a man when he is alive and not after he is dead. After that, let everything alone.

(WOLFSHEIM *waves and departs.*)

(NICK *notices a* MAN, *as he has noticed the* CREW *before during a transition. He moves casually to stand next to the man. They both seem to be window shopping at the same window.* NICK *may well be cruising, actually, though he may not be fully conscious of that and may well believe he has invented this behavior himself.*)

(*As* NICK *turns his head to check the man out, the man turns curiously toward* NICK *and it is* TOM. TOM, *who is always on the lookout for other people's feelings of humiliation, may know what is going on even less than* NICK, *but he senses that he has* NICK *at a disadvantage.*)

(TOM *raises an eyebrow and extends a hand to shake.* NICK, *deeply embarrassed without quite knowing why, does not respond.*)

TOM: What's the matter, Nick? Do you object to shaking hands with me?

NICK: You know what I think of you.

TOM: You're crazy, Nick, crazy as hell. I don't know what's the matter with you.

NICK: Tom, what did you say to George Wilson that night?

TOM: I told him the truth. What if I did? That Gatsby had it coming to him. He threw dust into your eyes just like he did in Daisy's, but he was a tough one. He ran over Myrtle like you'd run over a dog and never even stopped his car. And if you think I didn't have my share of suffering—look here, when I went to give up that flat and saw that damn box of dog biscuits sitting there on the sideboard, I sat down and cried like a baby. By God it was awful.

JORDAN: And you shook hands with him. *(She is there, watching.)*

(NICK does shake hands with TOM, and then TOM is gone, to rejoin DAISY in the billboard in the sky.)

NICK: It seemed silly not to. I felt suddenly as though I were talking to a child. They are careless people, Tom and Daisy—they smash up things and people and then retreat back into their money or their vast carelessness, or whatever it is that keeps them together, and let other people clean up the mess they've made...

JORDAN: Yes, well. You broke up with me on the telephone.

NICK: I...

JORDAN: You broke up with me on the telephone and you acted as if that was somehow what I deserved. I don't give a damn about you now, but it was a new experience for me, and I felt a little dizzy for a while. Do you remember a conversation we had once about driving a car?

NICK: Why—not exactly.

JORDAN: You said a bad driver was only safe until she met another bad driver? Well, I met another bad driver, didn't I? Careless of me. You said you were an honest person. But you are no better than any of the rest of us. You just think you're better. And that makes you worse. *(She ascends as well.)*

NICK: I'm...tremendously sorry.

(A moment of the sound and lights of the train again. Suddenly it is drowned out by a thunderous, slow, rhythmic knock, knock knock. The sound of knuckles on a door, and also of the rhythmic earth movers of the Valley of Ashes.)

(NICK turns.)

MR GATZ: Henry C Gatz. I come for the funeral of my son.

(Note: HENRY C GATZ, in coverall, coat, hat, and the weight of thirty years of greater age, is of course the raw image of his son. But this is the first character of consequence in the story who is not trying to seem to be something he is not. The gravitas that GATSBY aspired to, this man in his authenticity achieves without a thought. And because of that, he seems despite his age to be a character with more of the future in him than the younger man he has played until now.)

MR GATZ: Have I missed the funeral? I saw it in the Chicago newspaper. It was in all the Chicago newspapers. I started right away.

NICK: You came from Chicago?

MR GATZ: Dakota.

NICK: I didn't know how to reach you. Wouldn't you like some coffee?

MR GATZ: I don't want anything. I'm all right now, Mr—

NICK: Carraway.

MR GATZ: Well, I'm all right now. Where have they got Jimmy? May I see my son?

NICK: I didn't know what you'd want, Mr Gatsby—

MR GATZ: Gatz is my name.

NICK: I thought you might want to take the body West.

MR GATZ: Jimmy always liked it better down East. He rose up to his position in the East. Were you a friend of my boy's, Mr—?

NICK: We were close friends.

MR GATZ: He had a big future before him, you know. He was only a young man, but he had a lot of brain power up here. If he'd of lived, he'd of been a great man. He'd of helped build up the country.

NICK: You've heard…what happened? It was a madman. The man who killed him.

MR GATZ: Mm hm.

NICK: The police said. The coroner's inquest.

MR GATZ: I know what they said. It was in the papers.

NICK: The man who shot your son, he killed himself.

MR GATZ: White man. One of those Nordics.

(Beat)

NICK: Nobody knows quite why it happened.

(MR GATZ looks at NICK for a long time. NICK looks away.)

MR GATZ: Here's a thing I always carry. Jimmy sent me this. Look there.

NICK: It's a picture of this house.

MR GATZ: Jimmy sent it to me. It's a very pretty picture. It shows up well.

NICK: Very well.

MR GATZ: Of course we was broke up when he run off from home, but I see now there was a reason for it. He knew he had a big future in front of him. And ever since he made a success he was very generous with me.

NICK: Had you seen him lately?

MR GATZ: He come out to see me two years ago and he bought me the house that I live in now. Free and clear.

NICK: I suppose we should start.

(The CREW assembles the funeral: holding aloft on poles a canopy the color of ashes, at once like rainclouds, umbrellas, and a funeral home's pavilion.)

*(MR GATZ reluctantly puts away the picture, then pulls
from his pocket a ragged old copy of a dime novel titled
Hopalong Cassidy.)*

*(MR GATZ holds out his wrinkled souvenirs with the exact
gesture that GATSBY held out his. We can see, though
GATSBY never could, that he, far from having broken away
from this old man, could have been his true heir, and his
dream.)*

MR GATZ: Look here. This is a book he had when he
was a boy. It just shows you. *(Reading)*
"SCHEDULE, September 12, 1906.
Rise from bed, 6.00 A M
Dumbbell exercise and wall-scaling, 6.15-6.30
Study electricity, etc, 7.15-8.15
Work, 8.30-4.30 P M
Baseball and sports, 4.30-5.00
Practice elocution, poise and how to attain it, 5.00-6.00
Study needed inventions, 7.00-9.00
GENERAL RESOLVES No wasting time at Shafters or"
—some name I can't make out— "No more smoking
or chewing Bath every other day Read one improving
book or magazine per week Save $5.00—he crossed
that out and wrote $3.00—per week.
Be better to parents."
I come across this book by accident. It just shows you,
don't it? It just shows you. Jimmy always had some
resolves like this or something. Do you notice what
he's got about improving his mind? He was always
great for that. He never wanted anyone to think he was
lazy, or dirty, or that he hadn't worked for everything
he got, himself.
He told me I et like a hog once, and I beat him for it.

(A CREW member joins the little group, in a clerical collar.)

MINISTER: Blessed are the dead that the rain falls on.

(OWL-EYES *hurries in.*)

OWL-EYES: Amen to that. Sorry I couldn't get to the house.

NICK: Neither could anybody else.

OWL-EYES: Go on! Why, my God! they used to go there by the hundreds.

MINISTER: If anyone...has anything, that they would...?

(Beat)

NICK: I, ah...I have always tried to reserve judgment about people. It seemed a matter of infinite hope. Otherwise I am afraid I will miss something. But. My father told me once, and I have never forgotten it, that a sense of the fundamental decencies is parceled out unequally at birth. So I have to admit, my tolerance has a limit. These last months, life has been all riotous excursions, and a few privileged glimpses into the human heart. But today I want the world to come to attention, to be in uniform again, to be at a sort of moral attention forever. Except for Gatsby. Gatsby is exempt. Gatsby was everything I always...scorned. But...if personality is an unbroken series of successful gestures, then there was something gorgeous about him, some heightened sensitivity to the promises of life. He had an extraordinary gift for hope. A romantic readiness I have never found in any other person. It is not likely I shall ever find it again. What preyed upon Gatsby was...a foul dust floated in the wake of his dreams. Everyone else is all abortive sorrows and short-winded elations, and I just cannot... No. But Gatsby...Gatsby turned out all right at the end.

(MR GATZ *lays his hand on* NICK's *shoulder.*)

(NICK, *weeping, bows his head onto* MR GATZ's *shoulder.*)

(OWL-EYES *watches.*)

OWL-EYES: The poor son-of-a-bitch.

(The lights fade.)

END OF PLAY

www.ingramcontent.com/pod-product-compliance
Lightning Source LLC
Chambersburg PA
CBHW052128090426
42741CB00009B/2002